The Water and The Well: Encounters with God

A Wellspring Expressions Devotional

Arlesia M. Fortson

This
Devotional
Belongs
To:

Copyright

Copyright ©2022 Arlesia Fortson. All Rights Reserved. No part of this book may be reproduced in any form without permission from the author except as permitted by U.S. copyright law. To request permission, please contact Arlesia Fortson at Arlesia@wellspringexpressions.com

ISBN: 979-8-218-11952-2

Scripture quotations marked "ESV" are from the ESV Bible® (The Holy Bible, English Standard Version®), copyright © 2001 by Crossway Bibles, a publishing ministry of Good News Publishers. Used by permission. All rights reserved.

Scripture quotations marked (AMP) are taken from the Amplified Bible, Copyright © 1954, 1958, 1962, 1964, 1965, 1987 by The Lockman Foundation. Used by permission

Scriptures marked CJB are taken from the COMPLETE JEWISH BIBLE (CJB): Scripture taken from the COMPLETE JEWISH BIBLE, copyright© 1998 by David H. Stern. Published by Jewish New Testament Publications, Inc. www.messianicjewish.net/ jntp. Distributed by Messianic Jewish Resources Int'l. www.messianicjewish.net. All rights reserved.Used by Permission.

Scripture quotations marked "ASV" are taken from the American Standard Version Bible (Public Domain).

Scripture quotations marked "BSB" are taken from The Holy Bible, Berean Study Bible, BSB. Copyright ©2016, 2018 by Bible Hub. Used by Permission. All Rights Reserved Worldwide.

Scriptures marked GW are taken from the GOD'S WORD (GW): Scripture taken from GOD'S WORD® copyright© 1995 by God's Word to the Nations. All rights reserved.

Scriptures Quotations marked "GNB" or "GNT" are from the Good News Bible © 1994 published by the Bible Societies/HarperCollins Publishers Ltd UK, Good News Bible © American Bible Society 1966, 1971, 1976, 1992. Used with permission.

Copyright

Scriptures marked WEB are taken from the THE WORLD ENGLISH BIBLE (WEB): WORLD ENGLISH BIBLE, public domain. Scripture taken from the Holy Bible: International Standard Version®. Copyright © 1996-forever by The ISV Foundation. ALL RIGHTS RESERVED INTERNATIONALLY. Used by permission.

Scripture quotations marked "KJV" are taken from the Holy Bible, King James Version (Public Domain). Scripture quotations marked "NASB" are taken from the New American Standard Bible®, Copyright © 1960, 1962, 1963, 1968, 1971, 1972, 1973, 1975, 1977, 1995 by The Lockman Foundation. Used by permission.

Scripture quoted by permission. Quotations designated (NET) are from the NET Bible® copyright ©1996, 2019 by Biblical Studies Press, L.L.C. http://netbible.com. All rights reserved.

Scripture quotations marked (NIV) are taken from the Holy Bible, New International Version®, NIV®. Copyright © 1973, 1978, 1984, 2011 by Biblica, Inc.® Used by permission of Zondervan. All rights reserved worldwide. www.zondervan.com The "NIV" and "New International Version" are trademarks registered in the United States Patent and Trademark Office by Biblica, Inc.®

Scripture quotations marked (NIrV) are taken from the Holy Bible, New International Reader's Version®, NIrV® Copyright © 1995, 1996, 1998, 2014 by Biblica, Inc.® Used by permission of Zondervan. All rights reserved worldwide. www.zondervan.com The "NIrV" and "New International Reader's Version" are trademarks registered in the United States Patent and Trademark Office by Biblica, Inc.®

Scripture taken from the New King James Version®. Copyright © 1982 by Thomas Nelson. Used by permission. All rights reserved.

Scripture taken from The Expanded Bible. Copyright ©2011 by Thomas Nelson. Used by permission. All rights reserved. Scripture quotations marked (NLT) are taken from the Holy Bible, New Living Translation, copyright © 1996, 2004, 2007 by Tyndale House Foundation. Used by permission of Tyndale House Publishers, Inc., Carol Stream, Illinois 60188. All rights reserved.

Copyright

Scripture quotations marked (TLB) are taken from The Living Bible copyright © 1971. Used by permission of Tyndale House Publishers, Inc., Carol Stream, Illinois 60188. All rights reserved.

Taken from the Holy Bible: Easy-to-Read Version (ERV), International Edition © 2013, 2016 by Bible League International and used by permission.

Scripture quotations marked JUB (or JBS) are taken from the Jubilee Bible (or Biblia del Jubileo), copyright © 2000, 2001, 2010, 2013 by Life Sentence Publishing, Inc. Used by permission of Life Sentence Publishing, Inc., Abbotsford, Wisconsin. All rights reserved.

Scripture quotations marked (GNT) are from the Good News Translation in Today's English Version- Second Edition Copyright © 1992 by American Bible Society. Used by Permission.

Scripture quotations noted CEB are taken from the Common English Bible, copyright 2011. Used by permission. All rights reserved.

Scripture quotations marked CSB have been taken from the Christian Standard Bible®, Copyright © 2017 by Holman Bible Publishers. Used by permission.

Christian Standard Bible® and CSB® are federally registered trademarks of Holman Bible Publishers.

Scripture quotations marked "DARBY" are taken from the Darby Translation Bible (Public Domain).

Table of Contents

In Memory and Dedication	v
Foreword	vi
From Incidental To Intentional: A Testimony of an Encounter with God's Faithfulness	vii
Introduction to the Encounter Experience	xii

Encounters With God

Everlasting Valentine	1
Let's Start Here	5
The Original Document	9
What If They Were Wrong?	13
May I Borrow Your Pen?	17
Make A Right Turn When It Hurts?	22
176	26
The Condition Is Not The Counselor	31
The Plumb Line	35
Mary's Choice	39
Press Forward There's More	43
Presents or Presence	47
Go Back	51
I'm Here	55
Who Is My Mother?	59
An Encounter With God: The Remedy For Our Negative Experience	65
Trust	70
God Is: Immutable	75
Plan B	79
If You Say So	83
The Outcome	86
What Will You Call It?	89
In Conclusion	93
Thank You!	96
Love: Reverence and Obedience	98
The Great Gardener	103
I Want Off	107
Remember What You've Seen	112
Grace In This Place	116
Fill In The Blank	119
Forgive, It's All They Had To Give	123
I Forgave The Man Who Raped Me	126
Glory On Display	132
Your Impact Is Needed	136
How Will You Use What You Have Left?	140
The Secret Place	145
The Promise In The Wait	148
Faith That Will Amaze	152
Fight The Feeling, Persevere	156
He's Worth The Climb	160
We Can't Lose For Winning	164
I Will Be Single	168
Nevertheless, I'll Keep It	173
Our Perfect Example	178
Finish	182
Pour	186
It Is Good	189
Acknowledgements	190
About the Author	193
Connect With Us	194
Scripture Index	195

In Memory and Dedication

Samuel Thomas, Jr., Lois Minor, Catherine Gibson, Agutha Jackson, Earscine Taylor, Lorraine Pitchford, Norvel Daniels, Margaret Daniels, Sam Moss, Clara Wilson, and Cornelius Flowers, Jr.

I honor you and am grateful to God for your invaluable presence and the precious deposits of love you planted in my heart while you lived. Your legacy will remain in my heart forever.
I love you.

Foreword

"A Breath Of Fresh Air". At a very trying moment when we could feel the wear and tear of ministry, we had the pleasure of reading this awesome devotional and it was just as we described it in our opening statement, "A Breath Of Fresh Air". Knowing the author personally and witnessing her personal growth first hand over the years, I was overwhelmed with the level of knowledge and encouragement I received from this devotional. The author shares her heart and unselfishly pours out of her spirit all that God has downloaded within her. This devotional served as a constant reminder of the importance of having a daily hunger and thirst for God and the things of God. This devotional not only stirred our spirit and rekindled our hunger for God, but it motivated us to rise every morning giving God thanks in spite of the frailties of life. As a reader you will be challenged to encounter God and embrace His new mercy. As we continued reading we found ourselves many times at God's fountain of refreshing water, where the fresh wind of his spirit took us higher in His glory. Get ready to go on the journey of a lifetime, the journey to a new commitment. The writings of this devotional are so transparent that regardless of your age or level of maturity it will speak to your heart and give you the strength to go forward in God.

Apostle Larry B. and Pastor Olivia C.Q. Aiken
Memorial Church International

Arlesia Monique Fortson is truly a one of a kind young lady. She has overcome a number of things and still comes out on the other side, standing with her head held high. She is my greatest success in life. I thank God for her and I am truly blessed to have been your mother. I am blessed to have been able to watch her grow into the young lady she has become. I really can't find the words to express how special she is to me. I love her more than words can say, she is truly a blessing.

Debra Parks-Thomas
Mother

From Incidental To Intentional: A Testimony of an Encounter With God's Faithfulness

Look at what God has done! These things amaze us.
Psalms 66:5 (ERV)

One Monday night while driving to church, I watched a deer cross in front of my car. In the next instant, there was an impact and then excruciating pain. At that moment, I saw a second deer, a male, lying in the street. I watched him struggle, on broken limbs, to get across the street where he was able to run away into the darkness.

In the immediate moments to follow, I spoke to my loved ones, all while distracted by this pain, in my head, neck, and arm. My ability to respond became very delayed and as my husband arrived on the scene, I noticed that everything was slowing down. I would later learn that I had sustained a concussion.

My husband took me to the hospital where I was met by several medical professionals with several questions that were difficult to answer due to the intense pain, and my decreased ability to process information because of the concussion.

As I was being transported to get a CT scan, to check for internal injuries, The Holy Spirit whispered the words, "incidental finding." The CT scan was complete and I was returned to my room. As I lay flat, in a neck collar, the physician came and stood over me.

"Mrs. Fortson, we can take your collar off now. We did not find any internal injury to your brain or neck, but there was an incidental finding that has nothing to do with your accident. You need to see your doctor first thing in the morning. We discovered a mass." We left the emergency room and the ride home was filled with gratitude. My heart's declaration was "God thank you for this accident!"

The next morning was the first of many appointments. In the days to follow, I had to undergo several procedures, tests, imaging, bloodwork, scopes, biopsies, and consultations with two surgeons.

The initial report was as follows:

"Mrs. Fortson, you have a mass that originates in your neck and extends downward into your chest. We don't know what it is or how long it's been there, but it is pressing everything in your chest cavity downward. It is compressing your airway and the circulation to your heart.

If it had not been discovered 'incidentally', it would have been discovered emergently, as it continued to grow. The compression to your esophagus could have caused you to choke while you were eating. The compression to your airway could have caused you to stop breathing. The compression of the circulation to your heart could have caused a cardiovascular emergency.

You don't need to go to the operating room at this very moment, but you will need to go soon. This surgery will require both an ENT surgeon and a cardiovascular surgeon present in the operating room. We will coordinate our schedules and set a date."

The day of surgery arrived, and with my loved ones praying in the waiting room and all over the country, I entered the operating room. My understanding is that the wait was challenging, to say the least. Concern waxed and waned with every report from the operating room. The most concerning report being, "The saw is on the table, they may have to open her chest."

The surgery was completed and I was sent to post op to recover.

The final report was that the ENT surgeon had to remove half of my thyroid in order to get to the mass. It was more difficult to remove the mass than expected. It had grown to the size of my surgeon's fist, and had adhered itself to the surrounding tissues. In an effort to prevent opening my chest with a saw, the cardiovascular surgeon had to use force to pull my chest cavity away from my body to make room for all of the mass to be removed.

I asked God for three specific things as I prepared for surgery. I asked to keep half of my thyroid. I asked for my chest to not have to be opened with the saw. I asked for the mass to not be cancerous. He answered all of my prayers!

Recovery was painful. I have experienced natural childbirth, yet the pain that I experienced while recovering, pales in comparison to any contraction I have ever felt. However, in the midst of pain my declaration was, "Everyday has been better than the day before!" My declaration was not a denial of my circumstance but a reflection of my decision to focus on what matters most, my life.

The temporary pain I experienced was a blessing, because the alternative was death.

For this light momentary affliction is preparing for us an eternal weight of glory beyond all comparison,
2 Corinthians 4:17 (ESV)

There is no explanation of why the mass developed.

I did not have any known symptoms related to the mass, until 5 days prior to surgery.

I had been walking around living closer to death than I ever could have imagined.

I could have died while sleeping.

I could have died while on vacation with friends.

I could have died while singing in the choir.

I could have died while laughing with my children.

I could have died while embracing my husband.

I could have died while working in the intensive care unit.

I could have died while drinking my protein shake.

I could have died while on the treadmill.

I could have died.

BUT….GOD…..KEPT….ME!

Me, with all of my imperfections.

Me, with all the mistakes I've made.

ME!

Little..ole…me.

I owe God everything I am and I am forever changed. My surgical scar is in the shape of a capital T and it will be with me forever. I've been asked if I will be ashamed to show my scar to the world. My answer is never! Shame is not my portion! This T will forever represent the Testimony of God's faithfulness in sparing my life.

Thank you for allowing me to share my testimony with you. My encounter with God encouraged me to seek Him like never before. It encouraged me to live intentionally in service to Him, because He intentionally saved my life. It was a tangible display of how much He loves me, how He is keeping me when I don't realize I need to be kept, and that He is truly the source of everything I need. It is my prayer that the testimony of my encounter will encourage you to seek an authentic relationship with God and live a life completely surrendered to Him. A life lived on purpose, with purpose.

Arlesia Fortson

Introduction To The Encounter Experience

But those who drink the water I give will never be thirsty again. It becomes a fresh, bubbling spring within them, giving them eternal life."
John 4:14 (NLT)

This devotional serves as an invitation to be still with the God that satisfies the thirst of our longing soul. As you journey through this devotional I pray for a fresh encounter with God that results in authentic relationship, comfort, strength, encouragement, and maturity in every area of your life.

There are no time constraints regarding how you progress through this devotional so please take the time you need with each encounter and corresponding scripture. Each encounter has questions designed to encourage reflection on what you've read. In the creative space provided, take your time to respond to the questions and document what God shares with you in your own way. The creative space is designed for you to express your response by writing, drawing, coloring, highlighting, etc. However you feel led to document the details of what God speaks to your heart is the right way.

God is our source of all that we need. It is my prayer that your journey through the pages of this devotional will position you to encounter God as both the water and the well. The well from which we draw our strength, and everything that we need that pertains to life and godliness. The living water, our only source of true satisfaction and salvation. Drink from Him. He is the well that will never run dry.

Everlasting Valentine

For God so [greatly] loved and dearly prized the world, that He [even] gave His [One and] only begotten Son, so that whoever believes and trusts in Him [as Savior] shall not perish, but have eternal life.
John 3:16 (AMP)

Several years ago I took my son to a lab to have his blood drawn. His name was called and I carried him into this examination room decorated specifically for young children. The nurses educated me on the process. I was informed that both of his arms would be assessed, in order to determine the best source for the blood draw.

I laid my nine month old son on an exam table that folded down from the wall, similar to a changing table. He looked at me and smiled, comforted by my presence. The nurse proceeded to strap each of his arms to a board. Both arms were restrained straight out to his side.

Almost immediately, I was nearly overcome with emotion. One of the nurses attempted to comfort me. "It's ok. It will be quick. He will be fine." Although her intentions were pure, the nurse misunderstood the reason for my tears.

At that time, my son was my only child. My tears were not because he had to have blood drawn. I cried, because I understood in a brand new way.

As I looked into the eyes of my only begotten son, it clicked. My heart was overwhelmed by the depth of love and the magnitude of the sacrifice made for me.

With a tear stained face, I looked at him restrained in the position of the cross. As my mind processed how much I loved him, I could not fathom the idea of volunteering his life for the people in the room; let alone for the sins of the entire world.

Never breaking the gaze on my son, I silently confirmed in my heart, what God was fully aware of.

"God, you really gave your Son for me."

The blood was drawn. I removed the restraints, picked up my son, and I left with him.

God didn't make the same choice. He didn't remove the nails. He left His son on the cross to die for me, for you, for us, for them.

Let us never forget the greatest expression of love, God giving his only son to die in our place.

There is no greater love. It is because of that love, that He alone, is our Everlasting Valentine.

For Reflection

How can I live my life in gratitude for God's everlasting expression of His love for me?

Have I fully processed the truth that Jesus would have died for me even if I was the only person on Earth?

For Reflection

Let's Start Here

Then Christ will make his home in your hearts as you trust in him. Your roots will grow down into God's love and keep you strong. And may you have the power to understand, as all God's people should, how wide, how long, how high, and how deep his love is. May you experience the love of Christ, though it is too great to understand fully. Then you will be made complete with all the fullness of life and power that comes from God.
Ephesians 3:17-19 (NLT)

The beginning of anything is vitally important to the life and success of any endeavor. As believers, our new creation in Christ was established in the work of the cross; the greatest act of love toward us. This truth should be the beginning, the anchor, and the root, of everything we do as Christians.

Our focus scripture tells us that our roots grow down into God's love and keep us strong. As a result, we are anchored and overwhelmed by a love we will know from no other source.

A love that travels wide enough to embrace us.
A love that travels higher than any mountain that stands in our path.
A love that is longer than any trial can last.
A love that is deeper than the deepest heartache.

It is from this love, that we are complete, full, and lacking nothing.

When we are rooted in the overwhelming love of God we will not begin any endeavor, in an attempt to fill a void. Instead, our efforts will flow from the truth of being established and secure. We will enjoy God and walk in His purpose for our lives, from the security of love, not in the search of love.

When we are faced with plans to launch, restart, and reboot, let's start here, at the beginning, at the root of the matter.

The root of the matter is that we are fully complete in God and His love for us is overwhelming.

Now…..Let's get started.

For Reflection

Do I have projects, assignments, or endeavors that I have started but have not completed?

Are these projects rooted in the truth that I am already loved, and not the desire to be loved as a result of completing these endeavors?

Are there opportunities for me to reevaluate my being rooted in the truth that I am already complete in God, prior to the launch or restart of any future endeavors?

For Reflection

The Original Document

When someone becomes a Christian, he becomes a brand new person inside. He is not the same anymore. A new life has begun!
2 Corinthians 5:17 (TLB)

One of the first skills we learn in preschool is cut and paste. This skill is highlighted early in our education because the use of scissors helps to strengthen our hands to prepare for writing. We mature and grow and soon we begin to write. Before long, our writing transitions to typing. At this point, our cut and paste skills move from pen and paper, to the keyboard. While typing, we become familiar with cutting from the original document (control X) and pasting into a new document (control V).

Learning of God's character and love for us is, in most cases, very different from anything we've experienced in life. His unconditional love, lovingkindness, mercy, and grace, seem impossible to believe. In an effort to make it make sense, we employ one of the first skills we learned, cut and paste.

We cut the face of the person that represented love to us and paste it on the character of God.

If the experience was not pleasant, trusting God seems difficult at best.

This is how _____ treated me and they said they "loved" me, so this is what God means when He says He loves me.

If_____ was never dependable, God won't be either.

If_____ abandoned me, God just might do the same.

This mindset can happen when we misplace the original.

Entering into a relationship with Christ changes everything! As our focus scripture tells us, we are brand new in Christ. We are not the same.

This also means that our mindset changes. In Christ, we reference the character of God, and paste that truth into our present and future experiences:

"God loves me with an unfailing love. As a result I am able to love others regardless of how they treat me."

"God is always dependable. He will provide the resources and relationships to meet my needs in this season."

"God will never leave me nor forsake me. Should others decide to leave my life, God will comfort and strengthen me."

When we enter into a relationship with Christ, He becomes our standard, not our past experiences. We cut the standard for all life experiences from His character, and paste it into every situation. This aligns our perspective with heaven, protects our hearts, and prevents us from carrying unnecessary weight. Let us always keep God as the reference point, the standard, the original. Let us be careful to never misplace the original. God is the original document.

For Reflection

Are there areas of my life that I have compared God's character to past relationship experiences?

Are there opportunities to align my perspective of life and experience with heaven?

For Reflection

What If They Were Wrong?

For the word of God is living and active. Sharper than any double-edged sword, it pierces even to dividing soul and spirit, joints and marrow. It is able to judge the thoughts and intentions of the heart.
Hebrews 4:12 (BSB)

Has someone ever said something hurtful to you that took your breath away? The words that they spoke felt like a stab wound that was deep enough to have caused internal bleeding. Their words pierced your heart like a sword; so deep that you didn't believe that you would recover, but you did.

You healed, but you healed with the imprints of those words etched on your heart. The words have left behind rejection, abandonment, and hopelessness. To make matters worse, frustration became constant because, no matter how strong the effort, the words would not erase from your heart.

"Sticks and stones may break my bones, but words will never hurt me." is a common childhood phrase that has been found to be 100% false. Words do hurt. Words from people that hold significant roles in our lives seem to hurt worse. The words combined with the disappointment of the person speaking the words, can be difficult to comprehend.

Questions can begin to flood our thoughts:

Why would you say that to me?
That's how you feel about me?
Those are the words you use to describe me?

As painful as this experience can be, it's important to ask one more question. This question is self-directed.

What if they are wrong?

When words are spoken, they can cut deep. If this question is not asked we can go on to live a life based on wrong words spoken over our lives. If we live as though they were right, we live as if we are rejected, abandoned, and hopeless.

But.. What if they were wrong?

> *For the word of God is living and active. Sharper than any double-edged sword, it pierces even to dividing soul and spirit, joints and marrow. It is able to judge the thoughts and intentions of the heart.*
> *Hebrews 4:12 (BSB)*

There is a Word that will pierce our heart. The difference is that this Word heals and brings life. It can see what's really in our hearts and bring healing and correction in love. This Word will reach the deepest parts of our heart and erase the lies and replace them with truth. This Word provides a healing so deep and thorough that it motivates forgiveness.

This Word is the Word of God.

It is an unfortunate guarantee that in this life, someone will say something hurtful to us. However, we have an answer for healing. Instead of bleeding out over everything and everyone, we have to allow the Master Physician to heal us with His Word.

The Word of God will speak life and truth to our heart. When needed it will correct in love, and motivate maturity and growth in our relationship with Him. We must make the Word of God the standard, so the counterfeit words can be recognized when they are offered as truth in our lives.

For Reflection

Have I been wounded by the words of another? Am I still bleeding?

Do I believe that the words of God are able to heal my pain?

God's word is forever true, am I willing to make His word the standard for my life?

For Reflection

May I Borrow Your Pen?

My tongue is the pen of a ready writer
Psalms 45:1 (KJV)

Have you ever owned a pen that wrote extremely well? I mean it wrote so well that you were suddenly motivated to write, anything and everything. It's very likely that you kept the location of this high caliber pen classified; only to be used when absolutely necessary.

Then it happens, you are given a mission. The mission is to sign a document and return the pen to its safe location. The pen is retrieved from its classified location and the document is signed. The mission is almost completed! You are preparing to return the pen, and you hear the words "May I borrow your pen?"

With great hesitancy, you hand the pen over and try not to stare the entire time the pen is being used. There's a distraction, your attention is diverted from the pen, and when you return your glance….dunh dunh, dunh, the pen burglar and your pen are gone! Although comical, this is unfortunately a regular occurrence in the natural. The same theft, however, is occurring spiritually.

My tongue is the pen of a ready writer
Psalms 45:1 (KJV)

Death and life are in the power of the tongue: and they that love it shall eat the fruit thereof.
Proverbs 18:21 (KJV)

Scripture makes it clear that the tongue has power to author our detriment or our destiny, the choice is ours.

Life experiences can bring happiness, joy, and laughter. They may also bring anger, rejection, disappointment, and sadness. We get angry when someone intentionally hurts us or someone we love. We feel rejected when a beloved person walks away, and disappointed with unmet goals. Then there's the sadness felt, when we mourn the loss of a loved one.

When we neglect to take our broken heart to the cross to be healed by God; our emotions can place the matters of the heart on repeat, like a favorite song. The manifestation of this reality is evident to those closest to us, because oftentimes they hear the details of the experiences that hurt us, repeatedly, for days, months, or even years.

The truth is, it happened. The truth is, it hurt. The truth is, it wasn't your fault. The truth is, you didn't deserve it. It is also true that the pain you are experiencing does not compare to the glory of your future.

I consider that our present sufferings are not worth comparing with the glory that will be revealed in us.
Romans 8:18 (NIV)

We have an enemy whose goal is to abort our destiny. He desires for us to practice our pain, so that we never live to see the presentation of our future. His weapon of choice, our pen.

Above all else, guard thy heart; for out of it flows the issues of life.
Proverbs 4:23 (JUB)

Proverbs admonishes us to guard our hearts, because out of our hearts flow the issues of life. When we have issues of life, they most often flow, out of our heart, through our mouth. Another name for this "flow" is venting. We vent to verbally process how we are feeling at the moment. We are human, we have feelings, they get hurt. However, after the moment has passed, the enemy is waiting to ask the question "May I borrow your pen?" This is where our decision of detriment or destiny hangs in the balance.

The decision of detriment says:

"I am hurt, and I choose to keep my pain. I choose to never take it to God and allow Him to heal me. I choose to hold this pain close to me and talk about it, forever."

When this decision is made, we allow the enemy to borrow our pen, our tongue. With our pen we write death by verbally repeating our pain every day.

The decision of destiny says:

"Wow, I was not expecting this. I am broken in places I didn't know I could break. I will seek wise counsel from a trusted sister or brother in Christ and ask them to agree with me in prayer. I will take my brokenness to God and receive healing. I will say what God says about me and my situation, according to the Bible. I will speak life!"

When this decision is made, we keep our pen for our own use. We write life by speaking life, even when we don't "feel" like it and even before change has manifested in our situation.

When we make a decision to follow Jesus we can expect trials and tribulations, which means we can expect pain. Our responsibility is to guard our hearts, keep our pens, and write our destiny.

The righteous person faces many troubles, but the LORD comes to the rescue each time.
Psalms 34:19 (NLT)

For Reflection

What is my tongue writing?

Have I allowed the enemy to borrow my pen?

Are there opportunities for me to improve on how I guard my heart?

For Reflection

Make A Right Turn When It Hurts

Keep thy heart with all diligence; for out of it are the issues of life.
Proverbs 4:23 (KJV)

Have you ever experienced heartache? The type of heartache that can come from disappointment, discouragement, loss, or betrayal.

It's an indescribable pain that aches so deep that no human hand can reach.

The truth is, we will experience heartache, either intentionally or unintentionally. However, when we have decided to love God with all that we are; our response is to submit to the Word of God, no matter how we feel, even when our hearts hurt. When we don't we are more likely to respond from our pain, and that's dangerous.

Master, which is the great commandment in the law?

Jesus said unto him, Thou shalt love the Lord thy God with all thy heart, and with all thy soul, and with all thy mind.
Matthew 22: 36-37 (KJV)

When we submit to the Word of God at the place of pain, our heart turns right, instead of left at the crossroads. The sign for the right turn says:

"Even in my pain, I submit to the Word of God." In my pain, I choose to forgive. In my pain, I choose to rejoice."

On the contrary, the sign for the left turn says:

"In my pain, I choose my feelings." In my pain, I will seek revenge. In my pain, I will abort the calling and assignment for my life."

Truth is, God never promised that we would not experience pain. When we enter into a relationship with God, we have to be prepared to experience joy and pain. We have comfort in knowing that He will never leave us. He promises to deliver the righteous out of all afflictions.

We have a responsibility to keep watch over our hearts, because everything we do flows from what's happening in our heart. We have to constantly be in submission to the Word of God, so that when heartache hits, we will respond correctly, and make a right turn.

For Reflection

Am I experiencing emotional pain or heartache that is unresolved?

At the place of pain, have I turned left to respond in my feelings or right to submit to the word of God?

For Reflection

176

Psalms 119

Imagine being in a 15-minute-long conversation with someone about a book that is described as amazing, life giving, and life changing. By the end of the conversation, the book is expressed as being amazing in 176 different ways. 176!

Wow, by description alone, this book has made the cut for your reading list, and you can't wait to ask, "What is the name of this book?" The answer, "The best-selling book of all time, The Holy Bible."

The 119th division of Psalms is the longest chapter in the Bible. For 176 verses, it exclaims the weightiness, benefit, and wealth of information and provision that the Bible provides. To hear them read aloud, is believed to take approximately 15 minutes.

Let's take a look at the value of having a relationship with both God and His Word.

Life of integrity:
How blessed and favored by God are those whose way is blameless [those with personal integrity, the upright, the guileless], Who walk in the law [and who are guided by the precepts and revealed will] of the Lord.
Psalms 119:1 (AMP)

Blessings and favor:
Blessed and favored by God are those who keep His testimonies, And who [consistently] seek Him and long for Him with all their heart.
Psalms 119:2 (AMP)

Ability to live a pure life:
How can a young man keep his way pure? By keeping watch [on himself] according to Your word [conforming his life to Your precepts]
Psalms 119:9 (AMP)

Answer on how to avoid sin:
Your word I have treasured and stored in my heart, That I may not sin against You.
Psalms 119:11 (AMP)

Strength in grief:
My soul dissolves because of grief; Renew and strengthen me according to [the promises of] Your word.
Psalms 119:28 (AMP)

Freedom:
And I will walk at liberty, For I seek and deeply long for Your precepts.
Psalms 119:45 (AMP)

Comfort:
This is my comfort in my affliction, That Your word has revived me and given me life.
Psalms 119: 50 (AMP)

Direction:
I considered my ways And turned my feet to [follow and obey] Your testimonies.
Psalms 119:59 (AMP)

Good Judgment:
Teach me good judgment (discernment) and knowledge, For I have believed and trusted and relied on Your commandments.
Psalms 119:66 (AMP)

Revival:
I will never forget Your precepts, For by them You have revived me and given me life.
Psalms 119:93 (AMP)

Wisdom:
Your commandments make me wiser than my enemies, For Your words are always with me.
Psalms 119:98 (AMP)

Peace and stability:
Those who love Your law have great peace; Nothing makes them stumble.
Psalms 119:165 (AMP)

The 119th division of Psalms focuses solely on the Word of God. All 176 verses speak of the invaluable riches found in scripture. God has given us all we need to live upright and victorious in His Word. He has made the provision for success; we are now responsible to consume it and apply it to our lives. The Bible is timeless, living, and active. It will always be here to guide us, regardless of the situation or circumstance.

Your word is a lamp to guide me and a light for my path.
Psalms 119:105 (GNT)

For Reflection

Am I aware of the value of having a relationship with God and His word?

What are three scriptures that I can apply to the area of my life that I need the most direction for?

For Reflection

The Condition Is Not The Counselor

After this there was a feast of the Jews, and Jesus went up to Jerusalem. Now there is in Jerusalem by the Sheep Gate a pool, which is called in Hebrew, Bethesda, having five porches. In these lay a great multitude of sick people, blind, lame, paralyzed, waiting for the moving of the water. For an angel went down at a certain time into the pool and stirred up the water; then whoever stepped in first, after the stirring of the water, was made well of whatever disease he had. Now a certain man was there who had an infirmity thirty-eight years. When Jesus saw him lying there, and knew that he already had been in that condition a long time, He said to him, "Do you want to be made well?"
The sick man answered Him, "Sir, I have no man to put me into the pool when the water is stirred up; but while I am coming, another steps down before me."
Jesus said to him, "Rise, take up your bed and walk." And immediately the man was made well, took up his bed, and walked.
John 5: 1-9 (NKJV)

For 38 years or 13,870 days, the man in this passage of scripture had an infirmity. For 1,981 weeks, this man experienced the discomfort of his infirmity. He experienced 456 months worth of weakness and inability to take care of himself. He spent a total of 19,972,800 minutes of being counseled by his condition.

There is a difference from being counseled *in* our condition and counseled *from* our condition. While we are *in* our condition, it is always best for us to seek wise counsel. Wise counsel serves as a voice of reason. It provides destiny driven direction. It speaks life and wisdom to our condition. It will remind us that where we are is not who we are. Wise counsel will direct our gaze to the One that is able to heal, while we are awaiting our healing. It is wise counsel that prepares us for victory in warfare.

For by wise counsel you will wage your own war, And in a multitude of counselors there is safety.
Proverbs 24:6 (NKJV)

On the other hand, it is dangerous and unfruitful to seek counsel *from* our condition. This is unfortunately what the man, highlighted in this passage of scripture, had done. His infirmity literally directed every decision of his life. It counseled him on who he was not, where he couldn't go, what he could not do, and what he could not accomplish. The counsel from his condition, resulted in him believing that his situation was hopeless, and that healing was not an option for him.

When Jesus asked him " Do you want to be made well?" He summarized everything his condition told him. In other words, I can't be healed, there's no hope for me. I'm all alone. I'll never be healed because I can't move fast enough to get to my healing.

O Lord, you have searched me and known me! You know when I sit down and when I rise up; you discern my thoughts from afar.
Psalms 139:1-2 (ESV)

I am so grateful that we are known, right now in this moment, just as Jesus knew the man with the infirmity. He knew him when his infirmity caused him not only to sit down, but to lie down. While knowing him so well, he told him to "Rise, take your bed, and walk." The Bible says he was healed immediately.

Jesus, the wonderful counselor, discerned his thoughts of hopelessness from afar. He discerned the poor counsel his condition had provided and replaced it with the wise counsel he needed. One encounter with wise counsel, disintegrated the previous 38 years of infirmity.

Counsel is weighty and serious advice. It will cause great impact, either to our benefit or to our detriment. The counsel of our condition will always distort the reality of our destiny and encourage complacency. Whereas, choosing the weightiness of wise counsel, establishes our purpose in God. This choice positions us to always be maturing in the things of God, avoiding unnecessary delay, and focusing on our Magnificent Obsession, God our Father.

For Reflection

Are there any conditions that I am receiving counsel from? If so, how can I change my perspective to seek counsel from God while in my condition?

Who has God used to provide wise counsel for me?

Am I a source of wise counsel for others?

For Reflection

The Plumb Line

The whole Bible was given to us by inspiration from God and is useful to teach us what is true and to make us realize what is wrong in our lives; it straightens us out and helps us do what is right. It is God's way of making us well prepared at every point, fully equipped to do good to everyone.
2 Timothy 3:16-17 (TLB)

Comparison is what determines the plumb line by which we live. It is what we use to measure if we are straight and upright. But who are we comparing ourselves to?

When we compare ourselves to others, we may think "Well at least I am not doing what she's doing." or "At least I'm doing what he is not doing." In doing this, we use another created being as the reference for how we live, in relationship to God and others. The danger in this is astronomical.

We are all capable of error. Life experiences, and environmental circumstances in our family of origin, can create faulty character traits that cause us to live less than upright. Because of our humanity, all of us are an unreliable and inconsistent plumb line for anyone.

A plumb line is a weight that is suspended from a string that is used as a vertical reference to determine if what has been built is straight or upright. The plumb line uses the law of gravity to determine its accuracy and therefore does not change, even if the person using it does.

Every word of God is flawless; he is a shield to those who take refuge in him.
Proverbs 30:5 (NIV)

The word of God is the only perfectly accurate plumb line, and should therefore serve as our only place of comparison. When we align ourselves next to the plumb line of the scripture, it prevents us from thinking that we are better than our neighbor. It highlights opportunities for maturity, that comparison to our peers never will. When applied to our life, the Bible empowers us to operate consistently, regardless of our circumstances. It tutors us in the importance of living life according to faith and not our feelings.

The scriptures work as a spiritual chiropractor, aligning us in ways that comparison to others will never achieve. As children of God we are created in His image. Let us be forever mindful to use His word to align our lives, in word and in action; so that the image we present to the world is accurate. This is crucial, because when we stand before Him, there is only one image He wants to see and that is Himself.

For Reflection

Do I compare myself to anyone?

What opportunities are present in my life to align myself to the word of God?

For Reflection

Mary's Choice

As they went on their way, he entered into a certain village, and a certain woman named Martha received him into her house. She had a sister called Mary, who also sat at Jesus' feet, and heard his word. But Martha was distracted with much serving, and she came up to him, and said, "Lord, don't you care that my sister left me to serve alone? Ask her therefore to help me."
Jesus answered her, "Martha, Martha, you are anxious and troubled about many things, but one thing is needed. Mary has chosen the good part, which will not be taken away from her."
Luke 10:38-42 (WEB)

In biblical times, guests were most often welcomed into the home with a meal that, in most cases, included bread. Sometimes, the meal consisted of bread alone. In this scripture, Martha is found busy preparing a meal to serve to Jesus and the disciples.

Imagine for a moment.

Martha is in the kitchen kneading the dough, rolling the dough, building the fire, and placing the bread in the oven. Jesus is at her home, and the desire to prepare the best meal for Him becomes overwhelming. There is so much to do. It could take 2-3 hours just to make the bread. Martha becomes frustrated and overwhelmed with all there was to do.

Is it possible that Mary was aware of the same to-do list? After all, Mary would be accustomed to the amount of work that goes into preparing for guests.

Martha realizes "I have help, but she's sitting down, while I am working hard!" Her heart spills out, "Jesus, don't you care that Mary is not helping me? Are you going to make her get up and help me?"

Martha demonstrated award winning productivity in her service to those that were present. However, Mary chose to sit in the presence of the One that could teach her how to serve most effectively, in every area of life.

Martha wanted the bread to be perfect. She wanted to be sure that everything was prepared correctly for her guests.

Mary knew that physical bread was necessary. However, she also knew that she could not live on bread alone. Therefore, she sat at Jesus' feet to hear every word that proceeded out of the mouth of God.

Mary chose the Bread of Life.

Productivity, in the proper context is necessary, and has its place in our lives. However, no amount of doing for God, should ever take precedence of our being in relationship with Him.

Let us always remember, that everything that we do for God, should always be a result of the overflow of our relationship with God. His presence is the one thing that is needful. He is the good part.

For Reflection

What is my personal definition of productivity?

Is my productivity an overflow of my relationship with God?

How can I be intentional in prioritizing God as most important in my life?

For Reflection

Press Forward, There's More

I don't mean to say that I have already achieved these things or that I have already reached perfection. But I press on to possess that perfection for which Christ Jesus first possessed me. No, dear brothers and sisters, I have not achieved it, but I focus on this one thing: Forgetting the past and looking forward to what lies ahead, I press on to reach the end of the race and receive the heavenly prize for which God, through Christ Jesus, is calling us.
Philippians 3:12-14 (NLT)

In our walk with God, we will have repeated opportunities to gain a testimony of His goodness. Sometimes our testimonies are birthed from trials and tribulations. Sometimes they are birthed from great accomplishments and achievements. Regardless of how our testimony is obtained, we have to be intentional about moving forward in our relationship with God.

Whenever God moves in our lives and on our behalf, we should always respond with praise and thanksgiving. However, we don't stop there. God is infinite and He has no limits. Therefore, there is so much more of Him to experience.

Yes! He supplied our needs but there's more...

Yes! He called us to maturity through that painful situation but there's more....

Yes! He blessed us financially but there's more....

Yes! He highlighted some opportunities for growth but there's more....

Yes! He saved our lives but there's more...

Yes! He disciplined us when we were wrong but there's more...

Yes! He healed our bodies but there's more...

In relationship with God, our desire is to know Him more intimately with each passing day. His infinite nature makes it impossible to "arrive" in our capacity of knowing Him. Therefore, let us not confine the character of a timeless God, to the accomplishments, victories, and testimonies of yesteryear. Instead, let us press forward in great pursuit, because there's so much more of Him to experience. Let us pursue His heart, because knowing Him is our prize. He alone is our reward.

For Reflection

In what ways can I be intentional about knowing the Lord more intimately today than I knew Him yesterday?

For Reflection

Presence or Presents?

The one thing I want from God, the thing I seek most of all, is the privilege of meditating in his Temple, living in his presence every day of my life, delighting in his incomparable perfections and glory.
Psalms 27:4 (TLB)

Presence: the state or fact of being present, as with others or in a place.
Presents: gifts

Have you had the experience where a loved one professes the love they have for you only when they want something?

If this happens often enough, you begin to expect to hear their profession of love only when they want something. The truth is that it is our heart's desire to do what we can for them whenever possible. However, we would appreciate being told how much we are loved, just because, without an attached request. Given this perspective, let's consider how we approach God.

God is the one and only source for all we will ever need:

And my God will liberally supply (fill until full) your every need according to His riches in glory in Christ Jesus.
Philippians 4:19 (AMP)

As a good father, he wants to give us good gifts:

If ye then, being evil, know how to give good gifts unto your children, how much more shall your Father who is in Heaven give good things to them that ask Him?
Matthew 7:11 (KJV)

As a result, we confidently go to Him to obtain what we need. We often go to Him, professing our love, right before we ask for what we need or want. He loves us so much and will meet every need. However, is it possible that He would also like to, occasionally be told how much He is loved without an attached request?

When You said, "Seek My face," my heart said to You, "Your face, O LORD, I shall seek."
Psalms 27:8 (NASB)

To seek the face of God is to seek His presence. In His presence we can just be with Him and enjoy Him. We can tell Him how grateful we are for what He's done. We can praise Him for who He is. We can sing praises of adoration and honor unto Him. It is these times that we just desire His presence alone.

The young lions do lack, and suffer hunger: but they that seek the Lord shall not want any good thing.
Psalms 34:10 (KJV)

There are other times where it's necessary to seek His hand. When there is a need, and we are asking for Him to provide. We are asking Him to do what only He can do. We are approaching Him, to ask of Him, because He is our source. It is these times that we are in need of His provision, His gifts, His presents.

We have such an amazing heavenly father that longs to take care of His children. We can be confident that He will indeed take care of us. However, because we love Him, we should be mindful to not only seek His hand for presents. We should also be intentional about seeking His face, for His presence alone. Next time we are preparing to seek our heavenly Father, let's ask ourselves: Am I seeking Him for His presents or for His presence?

For Reflection

Have I considered the difference in seeking the face of God vs. the hand of God?

How can I be intentional about spending time with God for the purpose of just enjoying His presence and not seeking His presents?

For Reflection

Go Back

Every year Jesus' parents went to Jerusalem for the Passover festival. When Jesus was twelve years old, they went to the festival as usual. When the festival was over, they went home, but Jesus stayed in Jerusalem. His parents did not know about it. They traveled for a whole day thinking that Jesus was with them in the group. They began looking for him among their family and close friends, but they did not find him. So they went back to Jerusalem to look for him there.

After three days they found him. Jesus was sitting in the Temple area with the religious teachers, listening and asking them questions. Everyone who heard him was amazed at his understanding and wise answers. When his parents saw him, they wondered how this was possible. And his mother said, "Son, why did you do this to us? Your father and I were very worried about you. We have been looking for you." Jesus said to them, "Why did you have to look for me? You should have known that I must be where my Father's work is. (or in my Father's House)"

Luke 2:41-52 (ERV)

Mary, Joseph, Jesus, and a host of family and friends, traveled to attend the Passover festival as usual, and had begun to travel home. After one full day of traveling, his parents realized that Jesus wasn't with them.

One Day

For twenty-four hours, there was no hearing His voice, preparing His meals, or simply looking at His face. They thought He was present amongst family and friends, but he was not, so they went back. They returned to the last place that they were with Him personally; not the last place the family and friends were with Him.

Our relationship with Jesus is an individual one, therefore, when there is distance; we have to go back to where we last encountered Him. The place where our family and friends encountered Him last, may be different from ours. Furthermore, we have to go back to Him, because we are the ones that have moved, 100% of the time.

We must ask..
Where was the last place I heard His voice?
Where was the last place I saw Him active in my life?

Three Days
After seventy two hours, Jesus was found. He was found doing his Father's work in His Father's house. Three days without knowing where your 12 year old child is, is a big deal. It's an even bigger deal when that 12 year old is the Savior of the world.

When we enter into a relationship with Jesus Christ, we are afforded a priceless privilege, to be in constant communication with our Savior. He is the lover of our soul, our comforter, our healer, our deliverer, our friend, and wise counselor. We must always be sensitive to where He is and what He is doing. The cost of traveling through this life without Him is astronomical.

We must above all things protect, guard, and hold at the highest esteem, our relationship with Him; always regarding His presence and our time with Him, as priority one.

A lot can happen in three days. Our Savior hung, bled, died, and was resurrected in three days, for the remission of our sin. In that same amount of time, Jesus' presence or absence in our everyday life, can determine what will live, die, and be resurrected in our lives.

Check in.

If there is distance, go back, because His Presence is Precious.

Draw nigh to God, and he will draw nigh to you.
James 4:8a (KJV)

For Reflection

Is there distance between God and I right now?

When was the last time I spent quality time with Him?

What can I do right now to draw near to God?

For Reflection

I'm Here

Where can I go from Your Spirit?
Or where can I flee from Your presence?
If I ascend into heaven, You are there;
If I make my bed in hell, behold, You are there.
If I take the wings of the morning,
And dwell in the uttermost parts of the sea,
Even there Your hand shall lead me,
And Your right hand shall hold me.
Psalms 139:7-10, NKJV

I remember an instance where I walked into a situation where a woman was facing the possibility of her husband's death. There was chaos, noise, and about 30 people present, but all of those people were focused on her husband, not her. Another person and I escorted her to a quiet place. The other person had to leave, and then, it was us, and silence. Here I was with a stranger, in likely one of, if not the most life altering moments in her life. I thought of all I could say or offer to do, and all I said was "I'm here." She began to weep as she said "Thank you so much." As quickly as the moment began, it was over. She was beckoned away and I moved forward with my day. This moment was a reminder of the ministry of presence, a ministry God demonstrates daily in our lives.

Our focus scripture makes it clear that there is no physical or emotional place that we can go to escape the presence of God. When life makes us feel as though we're on cloud nine, He is with us. When sadness and disappointment create a darkness that seems to hide us from the world, He is there. When the next step in life requires a journey outside of the proverbial "box", He is there.

The ministry of presence brings both comfort and challenge. Comfort comes with knowing that no matter what lies ahead, God is present, even in the absence of people. The challenge lies in the reality of the requirement to do "it." Regardless if "it" means facing the death of a loved one or pursuing the opportunity of a lifetime.

God knows and cares about where we are and what we face. He is a loving God that understands our hearts in a way that no human can. This truth provides the strength to do "it" with forward progress, so that we don't become stagnant and complacent.

God's ministry of presence does not guarantee the absence of trials and difficulties. It does however, provide joy and strength as highlighted in the following passages of scripture.

You lead me in the path of life; I experience absolute joy in your presence; you always give me sheer delight.
Psalms 16:11 (NET)

Then he told them, "Go, eat rich foods, drink sweet drinks, and send portions to those who cannot provide for themselves. Today is a holy day for the Lord. Don't be sad because the joy you have in the Lord is your strength."
Nehemiah 8:10 (GW)

The ministry of presence is the availability to provide love, comfort and support with little to no words at all. Me saying "I'm here" to a complete stranger did not remove the reality of her situation. My prayer is that it provided a moment of comfort as she prepared to move forward to handle the untimely death of her husband.

God promises that he will never leave us or forsake us. Regardless of what life brings, He will always be there, providing love, comfort, and support; sometimes with little to no words at all. His presence is all the strength that's needed to do "it", to move forward, because after all, there's a prize to attain.

Brothers and sisters, I can't consider myself a winner yet. This is what I do: I don't look back, I lengthen my stride, and I run straight toward the goal to win the prize that God's heavenly call offers in Christ Jesus.
Philippians 3:13-14 (GW)

For Reflection

Take a moment to remember one time of being comforted by God.

What are some of the benefits of God's presence?

How can I operate in the ministry of presence?

For Reflection

Who Is My Mother?

Then God said, "Let us make humankind in our image, after our likeness, so they may rule over the fish of the sea and the birds of the air, over the cattle, and over all the earth, and over all the creatures that move on the earth." God created humankind in his own image, in the image of God he created them, male and female he created them. God blessed them and said to them, "Be fruitful and multiply" Fill the earth and subdue it!"
Genesis 1: 26-28a (NET)

Have you ever seen a person that looked a lot like someone else that you know? You are so certain that these two people are related, that you felt that you could confidently ask "Are you related to (enter name here)?" and they would answer "Well as a matter of fact, I am." This happened to me often while growing up.

When I was younger, my mother worked at the senior living facility where my great grandmother lived. After school, I would go there to spend time with my great grandmother until my mother's shift ended. A significant portion of my childhood was spent walking the halls of this facility. I volunteered with the activities department and helped with crafts and bingo. I have great memories of hanging out with my great grandmother and making friends that were usually at least a half century older than I was.

While walking the halls, I would often be stopped by a smiling face asking, "Who is your mother?" When I responded with my mother's name, the response was almost always, "I knew it! You look just like your mother." Although I had met several people over the time span of several years, there were still so many that I didn't know. It was often those I hadn't met that recognized me by looking like my mother, someone I am closely related to.

> *Then God said, "Let us make humankind in our image, after our likeness, so they may rule over the fish of the sea and the birds of the air, over the cattle, and over all the earth, and over all the creatures that move on the earth." God created humankind in his own image, in the image of God he created them, male and female he created them. God blessed them and said to them, "Be fruitful and multiply" Fill the earth and subdue it!"*
>
> Genesis 1:26-28a (NET)

God's design is for man and woman to bear the image of God, to have dominion over the earth, and to be fruitful and multiply. The family is to grow and be a representation of God on Earth.

However, as a result of sin, dysfunction has occurred in families, and this has negatively affected God's design. Fathers and mothers are estranged from their children and siblings are in constant strife. The pain seems to run deeper, when the MVP (most valuable people) in our lives are the source.

Family dysfunction can result in loneliness and a desire to isolate, in an effort to prevent future pain. The challenge with this coping mechanism is, the walls built to keep people out, are the same ones that keep people from coming in. Waiting at these walls, are well meaning, loving, genuine people, that are assigned to your life to show you real love, God's way.

I hear your heart....

"You don't understand, my mother did awful things to me!"
"My father was never around!"
"My sister caused the deepest pain imaginable and we don't talk anymore, and I'm perfectly OK with that!"
"My brother!...what brother? After what he did, he doesn't even exist to me!"
"My spouse abandoned me!"
"I don't have anyone, I'm alone in life."

Please understand, God is not caught off guard or without a solution to any problem that life presents. He was aware of the dysfunction that sin would bring into our families and he has provided an answer to our pain. This answer serves as the vehicle to move our destiny forward, when the pain of dysfunction surrounds us like quicksand.

Even if my mother and father abandoned me, the Lord will take me in.
Psalms 27:10 (NET)

This is good news! If you have experienced abandonment either intentionally or unintentionally, God promises to take you in.

"Great!" you say, "But where will He put me, now that He has me?"

I'm glad you asked.

The God who is in his holy dwelling place is the father of the fatherless and the defender of widows. God places lonely people in families. He leads prisoners out of prison into productive lives, but rebellious people must live in an unproductive land.
Psalms 68:5-6 (GWT)

According to this scripture, God promises to place the lonely with families. To be able to recognize our opportunity for healing, we have to realize that the family He places us in, may be with people we are related to but don't physically look like.

Christ's shed blood, made His spiritual DNA available to all that receive the gift of salvation. With our salvation, we gain a family in Christ.

It is an unfortunate truth that sometimes, members of the family we are born into, are the cause of our pain. However, because we are created for relationship, God will supplement the family that we are related to by blood, with a family that we are related to by the blood of Jesus; when we accept Him as our Lord and Savior. As we are healed by His love and grace toward us, we begin to spiritually look like Jesus.

In Matthew 12:47-50 (CSB) someone told Jesus, "Look, your mother and your brothers are standing outside, wanting to speak to you." He replied to the one who was speaking to him, "Who is my mother and who are my brothers?" Stretching out his hand toward his disciples, he said, "Here are my mother and my brothers! For whoever does the will of my Father in heaven is my brother and sister and mother."

As a family in Christ, we begin to resemble one another as we live intentionally to resemble Him. We are intentional to live our lives, to look like the one who placed our lonely hearts in a family. We share with others about the room that is available in our family. We share because we have known and experienced the healing love of our Father and we want others to know that same love.

By this everyone will know that you are my disciples, if you love one another.
John 13:35 (NIV)

For Reflection

As a Christian, do I believe that I was created in the image of God?

Do I have hurt caused by my biological family that I need to allow God to heal?

Are there opportunities to deepen my relationship with my family in Christ?

For Reflection

An Encounter With God: The Remedy For Our Negative Experience

Don't remember these earlier events; don't recall these former events. Look, I am about to do something new. Now it begins to happen! Do you not recognize it? Yes, I will make a road in the desert and paths in the wilderness.
Isaiah 43:18-19 (NET)

On March 23, 2015 my dad went to the emergency room for stomach pain and trouble breathing. He was admitted to the hospital and his gallbladder was removed on his birthday, two days later. After surgery we were informed that he had cancer. My dad declined treatment and decided to transition to hospice and was soon discharged to the hospice house. During my time with him there, we spent hours together eating strawberry ice cream, watching baseball, and talking about everything.

After a time, he was discharged from hospice and went to rehab to get stronger. He gave the rehab therapists the hardest time. We would laugh when I would encourage him to participate in therapy. He would say, "I wasn't in this good of shape before I got sick." My dad wanted nothing more than to go home. After a while, he was able to go home to the house he and my mother shared. There we would stay up late, watching marathon episodes of Family Feud and you guessed it, more baseball. I didn't complain because I didn't know how many more days I had with him.

On a Saturday evening, we transferred him back to the hospice house to make him more comfortable, with the hope to return home soon. After a few days we were given the report that it was unlikely that he would return home. One week and one day later, this daddy's girl, held her father's hand and sang the song "For Your Glory" by Tasha Cobbs-Leonard, as he took his last breath and transitioned from Earth to Heaven. On September 6, 2015, I experienced the death of my father.

Experience: an event or occurrence that leaves an impression on someone.

Painful experiences, like the death of a loved one, can leave an impression on our heart and mind. These impressions can negatively govern and guide our life moving forward, if we are not introduced to something new.

The death of loved ones in my past, left the impression of pain, sadness, and heaviness on my heart. Had I relied on my past experiences with death, I could have easily been prepared to expect the same or worse with the passing of my father. However, during the time of my father's illness and eventual death, I encountered something different. Peace.

Encounter: an unexpected meeting with something or someone

In the midst of one of the most difficult times of my life, I did experience pain and sadness. However, this time there was a peace that I could not describe. The unwavering peace of God kept me.

Do not worry about anything; instead pray about everything. Tell God what you need, and thank him for all he has done. Then you will experience God's peace, which exceeds anything we can understand. His peace will guard your hearts and minds as you live in Christ Jesus.
Philippians 4:6-7 (NLT)

This peace I encountered was unexplainable. It interrupted my experience of what grief was supposed to be in that moment. The peace of God strengthened me to walk through the illness and death of my father. It strengthened me to deliver his eulogy. I encountered the Prince of Peace.

Don't remember these earlier events; don't recall these former events. Look, I am about to do something new. Now it begins to happen! Do you not recognize it? Yes, I will make a road in the desert and paths in the wilderness.
Isaiah 43:18-19 (NET)

Had I allowed what I remembered about my past experiences of death and grief to guide me at the time of my father's death, I would have missed my encounter. I would have missed the new thing that God did in my heart. My encounter with the Prince of Peace reveals the importance of always expecting God to do a new thing, no matter how dry and desolate the situation may seem.

Life happens. The good and the bad. When life offers negative experiences, let us not respond based on what we remember happening the last time. Let us be careful to recognize God's ability to change the course of our destiny, even if He has to make a road in a desert place.

For Reflection

Are there past negative experiences that I have allowed to guide my forward movement in life?

Take a moment to reflect on encounters that you have with God.

Am I willing to allow my encounter with God to guide my destiny, regardless of past experiences?

For Reflection

Trust...

But he had to pass through Samaria. Now he came to a Samaritan town called Sychar, near the plot of land that Jacob had given to his son Joseph. Jacob's well was there, so Jesus, since he was tired from the journey, sat right down beside the well. It was about noon. A Samaritan woman came to draw water. Jesus said to her, "Give me some water to drink." (For his disciples had gone off into the town to buy supplies.) So the Samaritan woman said to him, "How can you—a Jew—ask me, a Samaritan woman, for water to drink?" (For Jews use nothing in common with Samaritans.) Jesus answered her, "If you had known the gift of God and who it is who said to you, 'Give me some water to drink,' you would have asked him, and he would have given you living water." "Sir," the woman said to him, "you have no bucket and the well is deep; where then do you get this living water? Surely you're not greater than our ancestor Jacob, are you? For he gave us this well and drank from it himself, along with his sons and his livestock."

Jesus replied, "Everyone who drinks some of this water will be thirsty again. But whoever drinks some of the water that I will give him will never be thirsty again, but the water that I will give him will become in him a fountain of water springing up to eternal life." The woman said to him, "Sir, give me this water, so that I will not be thirsty or have to come here to draw water." He said to her, "Go call your husband and come back here." The woman replied, "I have no husband." Jesus said to her, "Right you are when you said, 'I have no husband,' for you have had five husbands, and the man you are living with now is not your husband. This you said truthfully!" The woman said to him, "Sir, I see that you are a prophet. Our fathers worshiped on this mountain, and you people say that the place where people must worship is in Jerusalem." Jesus said to her, "Believe me, woman, a time is coming when you will worship the Father neither on this mountain nor in Jerusalem. You people worship what you do not know. We worship what we know, because salvation is from the Jews. But a time is coming—and now is here—when the true worshipers will worship the Father in spirit and truth, for the Father seeks such people to be his worshipers. God is spirit, and the people who worship him must worship in spirit and truth." The woman said to him, "I know that Messiah is coming" (the one called Christ); "whenever he comes, he will tell us everything." Jesus said to her, "I, the one speaking to you, am he"

John 4: 4-26 (NET)

This scripture tells the story of Jesus, tired from the journey, choosing to make a detour. His detour is to minister to a woman that was considered an outcast, because of her immoral lifestyle. Not only that, as a Jew, it was prohibited for Him to even speak to her. Nevertheless, he was intentional about meeting with her and offering her living water. He took the time to see her, minister to her in her current situation, and offer her eternal life. He did this when no one else would, and when no one else was around.

Integrity: the soundness of moral character; who you are when no one is looking.

According to verse 8, the disciples had left Jesus alone to go into town. Jesus' encounter with the woman at the well, happened when no one was looking.

This encounter displayed His character. It revealed His desire and ability, to give what was needed, at the right time. She, as we all do, needed eternal life.

Jesus' choice to meet the need of one woman, in a private, life altering, encounter, is proof that He embodies the definition of integrity.

Trust: reliance on the integrity, strength, and ability, of a person or thing.

This passage of scripture reveals God's heart toward us.

It proves that regardless of what we've done, we are valuable to Him.

It proves that we can rely on His integrity.

It proves that we can trust Him.

Just as God sent Jesus to the woman at the well to offer her eternal life; He sent Jesus to die in our place, so we can have eternal life. Through Jesus Christ's death, burial, and resurrection, we can trust Jesus as Lord and Savior of our lives. We trust Him to have complete authority and control over our lives. In doing so, we trust that God's will is always in our best interest, no matter what.

Trust God? Yes and Always.

His intentions toward us are always pure.

We can rely on His integrity. He. Is. Trustworthy.

For Reflection

Has my experience with trust been positive or negative?

Have I attributed that experience to my ability to trust God?

Do I believe that God's intentions toward me are pure?

Are there opportunities in my life for me to trust God more than I do at this moment? If so, what are they?

For Reflection

God Is: Immutable

Jesus Christ the same yesterday, and today, and forever.
Hebrews 13:8 (KJV)

Immutable: Changeless; Unable to change

God.Never.Changes.

He will always take care of us:

I was young and now I am old, yet I have never seen the righteous forsaken or their children begging bread.
Psalms 37:25 (NIV)

The counsel of the LORD stands forever, the plans of his heart from generation to generation.
Psalms 33:11 (CSB)

He will always be with us:

But the Lord is the one who is marching before you! He is the one who will be with you! He won't let you down. He won't abandon you. So don't be afraid or scared!"
Deuteronomy 31:8 (CEB)

For this reason, we don't have to concern ourselves with the unknown. He is never surprised by what happened, nor will he be unprepared for what's coming.

If uncertainty arises about today, remember who God was yesterday. If the cares of tomorrow attempt to creep into our present, focus on who He is right now.

With intentional application of the truth that God never changes, all questions will quickly turn into declarations.

"Come what may, God will be there, in every circumstance."

"God is prepared to take care of all things concerning me, because He is the beginning and the end of all things"

It is God's immutability, His consistency, His faithfulness, that produces confidence in us.

A confidence that produces rest.

We can rest assured that He will always be God, and in Him is everything we will ever need.

For Reflection

In what ways can God's immutability produce confidence, peace, and rest in my life?

Do I trust that He is prepared to take care of all things concerning me? If not, why?

Do I believe that the unknowns of my life are not a challenge for God because of His immutable character? If not, why?

Am I fully convinced that God's intentions toward me are pure and will never change? If not, why?

For Reflection

Plan B

For I know the plans that I have for you,' declares the LORD, 'plans for well-being, and not for calamity, in order to give you a future and a hope.
Jeremiah 29:11 (ISV)

Plan B : a strategy or plan to be implemented if the original one proves to be unsuccessful.

We've all had one, a plan B. A self made insurance policy to protect ourselves in case something happens to plan A. Generally speaking, it is wise to have a plan.

We should plan to:
- have insurance coverage in life and in death.
- save for emergencies.
- have our umbrella on our person and not in the car, when rain is in the forecast.
- fill up the gas tank when the light first comes on, not after the 25 mile commute to work.
- have an extra change of clothes for the extra change of clothes, with all children four and under.

Although some planning is absolutely necessary, when it comes to the matters of the heart, having a plan B can be detrimental. As our hearts are concerned, we can develop a plan B after we have experienced failure on some level with the original plan. A failed relationship, the loss of a loved one, a loss of employment, a failed dream, the list goes on and on.

In an effort to prevent ourselves from having those experiences again, we develop plan B. Unfortunately, it can sometimes cause us to turn 180 degrees away from our destiny.

"I barely survived that, so I will not do that again."

"I won't love again."

"I won't dream again."

"I'd rather not do it, than suffer the pain of failing again"

When we fail, we tend to choose plan B because it seems to be the safe plan, but it's not. As it pertains to our relationship with God, we are to choose faith, not safe.

God is trustworthy. When we trust Him with our life, we don't need a plan B. He takes good care of His children. Even in failure, we will know success, because He has our best interest at heart. According to Romans 8:28, all things will work together for our good. We can take a deep breath and rest in that truth. We must take on an active part in our destiny, however, we are not responsible for our destiny. We are the builders but God is the architect. We can trust His plan because he sees the big picture.

For I know the plans that I have for you,' declares the LORD, 'plans for well-being, and not for calamity, in order to give you a future and a hope.
Jeremiah 29:11 (ISV)

For Reflection

Do I have a plan B for my destiny in an attempt to protect myself from pain and/or failure?

Do I believe God to be trustworthy?

Do I believe God has my best interest at heart?

Am I willing to trust God with the "big picture" of my life?

For Reflection

If You Say So..

One day as Jesus was preaching on the shore of the Sea of Galilee, great crowds pressed in on him to listen to the word of God. He noticed two empty boats at the water's edge, for the fishermen had left them and were washing their nets. Stepping into one of the boats, Jesus asked Simon, its owner, to push it out into the water. So he sat in the boat and taught the crowds from there.
When he had finished speaking, he said to Simon, "Now go out where it is deeper, and let down your nets to catch some fish."
"Master," Simon replied, "we worked hard all last night and didn't catch a thing. But if you say so, I'll let the nets down again." And this time their nets were so full of fish they began to tear! A shout for help brought their partners in the other boat, and soon both boats were filled with fish and on the verge of sinking.
Luke 5:1-7 (NLT)

Simon was a skilled fisherman and likely had been for a great majority of his life. At the time of this scripture, the fishermen had worked hard with no success, just the night before. Jesus' command was to do exactly what they had done the night before. Simon was sure to let Him know that he'd already tried that. However, instead of resisting the instructions, he simply said "If you say so, I'll do it."

Had Simon decided not to listen to Jesus, he would have missed the abundance of fish that was caught. There were so many fish, he had to call for help to handle the overflow. It is unlikely that he would have caught the same amount of fish in his own strength, the night before. It would have taken much longer to achieve the same result.

It is a blessing to receive education and training in various areas, however, the voice of God is priceless. His voice is always the first choice, the right choice, the only choice.

When God speaks, let's make a decision to respond "If You say so, I'll do it," regardless of what it looks like, because we can trust what heaven speaks.

For Reflection

Have I followed every instruction that God has given me?

Am I willing to commit to obeying God regardless of my feelings or opinion?

For Reflection

The Outcome

Let not your heart be troubled; you believe in God, believe also in Me.
John 14:1 (NKJV)

Jesus shared with the disciples that He would be betrayed and that he would be leaving them soon. He then commands them not to allow their hearts to become distressed or anxious.

This command is significant because action initiated from an anxious heart looks for ways to control the outcome. Knowing that the life altering information He shared with the disciples could induce anxious action, Jesus presents them with an alternative action. "You believe in God, believe also in Me."

Jesus presents the action of faith. He invites the disciples to have faith in His reliability by telling them to believe. This same invitation is available to us now. When faced with life altering circumstances, let us choose faith. Let's not attempt to control the outcome with anxious action powered by our own strength. Instead, let us move forward in faith filled action, knowing that the God that we trust is reliable. He not only controls the outcome, He is the outcome.

I am the Alpha and the Omega.
I am the First and the Last.
I am the Beginning and the End.
Revelation 22:13 (NIRV)

For Reflection

When life happens, do I lean more toward anxious action or faith filled action?

How has God proven Himself reliable in my past? How can I carry that memory forward into my current situation?

In what areas can I increase my faith filled action?

For Reflection

What Will You Call It?

Some time later, God tested Abraham's faith. "Abraham!" God called.
"Yes," he replied. "Here I am."
"Take your son, your only son—yes, Isaac, whom you love so much—and go to the land of Moriah. Go and sacrifice him as a burnt offering on one of the mountains, which I will show you."
The next morning Abraham got up early. He saddled his donkey and took two of his servants with him, along with his son, Isaac. Then he chopped wood for a fire for a burnt offering and set out for the place God had told him about. On the third day of their journey, Abraham looked up and saw the place in the distance. "Stay here with the donkey," Abraham told the servants. "The boy and I will travel a little farther. We will worship there, and then we will come right back."
So Abraham placed the wood for the burnt offering on Isaac's shoulders, while he himself carried the fire and the knife. As the two of them walked on together, Isaac turned to Abraham and said, "Father?"
"Yes, my son?" Abraham replied.
"We have the fire and the wood," the boy said, "but where is the sheep for the burnt offering?"
"God will provide a sheep for the burnt offering, my son," Abraham answered. And they both walked on together.
When they arrived at the place where God had told him to go, Abraham built an altar and arranged the wood on it. Then he tied his son, Isaac, and laid him on the altar on top of the wood. And Abraham picked up the knife to kill his son as a sacrifice. At that moment the angel of the Lord called to him from heaven, "Abraham! Abraham!"
"Yes," Abraham replied. "Here I am!"
"Don't lay a hand on the boy!" the angel said. "Do not hurt him in any way, for now I know that you truly fear God. You have not withheld from me even your son, your only son."
Then Abraham looked up and saw a ram caught by its horns in a thicket. So he took the ram and sacrificed it as a burnt offering in place of his son. Abraham named the place Yahweh-Yireh (which means "the Lord will provide"). To this day, people still use that name as a proverb: "On the mountain of the Lord it will be provided."
Genesis 22:1-14 (NLT)

Imagine that one thing, one person, one dream, one desire that holds great value. The one thing that you've worked hard to achieve and dreamt of your entire life. What would be your response if God asked you to sacrifice it? Would you allow your flesh to respond by holding it tight to your chest in resistance? Or would you allow faith to respond in worship?

Sacrifice: an act of giving up something valued for the sake of something else regarded as more worthy.

God asked Abraham for something of great value, his promised son, Isaac. Instead of tightening his grasp, Abraham released him. God called it sacrifice. Abraham called it worship.

"The boy and I will travel a little farther. We will worship there, and then we will come right back."

Worship comes from the word worth-ship. Worshiping God is regarding His worth as higher than anything else. As much as he valued his son Isaac, God was worth more. Abraham, believed God. He allowed his faith to respond. God's instruction for his life was worth letting go of his answered prayer. He believed above all things, that there is nothing in life, greater than God.

When we choose to believe God, we trust that He is God in all circumstances, even when it doesn't make sense; even when the cost of obedience seems great.

When we see God's worth, as priceless, responding in faith is the only choice. We know that no matter what, God will be God, He will make a way.

When God calls for a sacrifice. When He asks us to release our most prized possession; let us not respond in our flesh. Let us release it in faith, and call it worship, being careful to always value God above all things. He is worthy and He will provide.

For Reflection

What is one thing that holds great value to me?

What would my response be if God asked me to give it up?

Do I trust that God's instructions are always for my interest?

Is there something that God has asked me to release to Him? Am I willing to release it in faith?

For Reflection

In Conclusion

The end of a thing is better than its beginning;
Ecclesiastes 7:8a (NKJV)

Regardless of the challenges we may face in any given year, the conclusion of the year is better than the beginning. It is better because we are privileged to see God in ways we had not seen Him when the year began. By the end, we will have had 365 opportunities to see God be God, in ways we've never experienced. For 365 days He will be our strength, our provider, our comfort, our protector, our joy, and our peace. God is infinite and will never exhaust His ability to show Himself mighty in our lives. As we navigate through our 365 days, let us live in great expectation for what He will do and give Him great praise for what He has done.

For you are great, and do wondrous things. You are God alone.
Psalms 86:10 (NKJV)

For Reflection

God is always good. What is something that God has done that I can praise Him for?

What are three ways that God has kept me?

How have I grown as a result of God's character in my life?

What is something that I am expecting of God?

For Reflection

Thank You!

O God, I will offer you what I have promised; I will give you my offering of thanksgiving
Psalm 56:12 (GNT)

Go through his open gates with great thanksgiving; enter his courts with praise. Give thanks to him and bless his name.
Psalm 100:4 (TLB)

Always give thanks for everything to our God and Father in the name of our Lord Jesus Christ.
Ephesians 5:20 (TLB)

The Lord strengthens and protects me; I trust in him with all my heart. I am rescued and my heart is full of joy; I will sing to him in gratitude.
Psalm 28:7 (NET)

Keep your roots deep in him, build your lives on him, and become stronger in your faith, as you were taught. And be filled with thanksgiving.
Colossians 2:7 (GNT)

The peace that Christ gives is to guide you in the decisions you make; for it is to this peace that God has called you together in the one body. And be thankful.
Colossians 3:15 (GNT)

Be persistent and devoted to prayer, being alert and focused in your prayer life with an attitude of thanksgiving.
Colossians 4:2 (AMP)

In every situation [no matter what the circumstances] be thankful and continually give thanks to God; for this is the will of God for you in Christ Jesus.
1 Thessalonians 5:18 (AMP)

Give thanks to the Lord and call out to him! Tell the nations what he has done!
1 Chronicles 16:8 (ERV)

Give thanks to the Lord, because he is good. His faithful love continues forever.
1 Chronicles 16:34 (NIRV)

Thank You!

It is a good thing to give thanks unto the Lord, and to sing praises unto thy name, O Most High:
Psalm 92:1 (KJV)

But I will give great thanks to the Lord with my mouth; among a great crowd I will praise God!
Psalm 109:30 (CEB)

Give thanks to him who alone does mighty miracles. His faithful love endures forever.
Psalm 136:4 (NLT)

saying, "Amen! Blessing and glory and majesty and wisdom and thanksgiving and honor and power and might belong to our God forever and ever. Amen."
Revelation 7:12 (AMP)

I thank Christ Jesus our Lord, who has granted me [the needed] strength and made me able for this, because He considered me faithful and trustworthy, putting me into service [for this ministry],
1 Timothy 1:12 (AMP)

But we thank God! He gives us the victory through our Lord Jesus Christ.
1 Corinthians 15:57 (EXB)

I will praise the name of God with a song, and will magnify him with thanksgiving.
Psalm 69:30 (KJV)

Since we are receiving a Kingdom that is unshakable, let us be thankful and please God by worshiping him with holy fear and awe.
Hebrews 12:28 (NLT)

Thanks be to God for His indescribable gift.
2 Corinthians 9:15 (CSB)

Thanks be to the Lord, who daily carries our burdens for us. God is our salvation.
Selah
Psalm 68:19 (GW)

Love: Reverence and Obedience

Teacher, which is the greatest commandment in the Law?" And Jesus replied to him, "'You shall love the Lord your God with all your heart, and with all your soul, and with all your mind.' This is the first and greatest commandment.
Matthew 22:36-38 (AMP)

The question was asked of Jesus, "What is the greatest commandment?" and the answer was to love God with everything that we are. Our love in action does not exclude our human nature of having feelings, thoughts, and actions. It simply requires us to submit all of them to God. This truth causes us to evaluate our heart, in our declaration of "God, I love you!"

"If you [really] love Me, you will keep and obey My commandments.
John 14:15 (AMP)

The greatest commandment is to love God with all of our heart (our feelings), soul (what we will to do), and mind (how we think). In our love for God, we are to affectionately reverence Him in all that we feel, do, and think; and then obey quickly.

We may feel angry, but in our love for God we will declare:

"God, in my love for you, I choose to reverence you in how I feel."

"Your Word says..."

If you are angry, don't sin by nursing your grudge. Don't let the sun go down with you still angry—get over it quickly;
Ephesians 4:26 (TLB)

"In response to Your Word, I will obey quickly. I will feel how I feel and let it go."

We may want to do to them what they did to us, but in our love for God we will declare:

"God, in my love for you, I choose to reverence you in my actions."

"Your Word says..."

Dear friends, never take revenge. Leave that to the righteous anger of God. For the Scriptures say, " I will take revenge; I will pay them back," says the Lord.
Romans 12:19 (NLT)

"I will obey quickly. I will be still and let you handle it."

When there is negativity in our thought patterns, our love for God will cause us to declare:

"God, I choose to reverence you in my thoughts."

"Your Word says:"

Finally, believers, whatever is true, whatever is honorable and worthy of respect, whatever is right and confirmed by God's word, whatever is pure and wholesome, whatever is lovely and brings peace, whatever is admirable and of good repute; if there is any excellence, if there is anything worthy of praise, think continually on these things [center your mind on them, and implant them in your heart].

Philippians 4:8 (AMP)

" I will obey quickly. I will fix my thoughts on the truth of your Word."

Loving God with how we feel, what we do, and how we think, is the greatest commandment. To fulfill this commandment, our love will require great action and focused intention. Regardless of the cost, it is worth it, because He loved us first. God demonstrated His love by giving His son. Jesus demonstrated His love by giving His life. In response to the opportunity to be in right relationship with God, reverence and obedience is the very least we can do. He's so worthy!

For Reflection

Do I love God with all my heart, soul, and mind?

What opportunities are present for me to demonstrate my love with my feelings, thoughts, and actions?

For Reflection

The Great Gardener: Pruned To Produce

I am the true vine, and my Father is the gardener. Every branch in me that does not produce fruit he removes, and he prunes every branch that produces fruit so that it will produce more fruit.
John 15:1-2 (CSB)

Prune: to take away anything that is unnecessary and excessive that hinders growth and fruitfulness, in order to increase future growth.

As it pertains to gardening, pruning occurs regularly and is an extremely vital part of plant health. However, the timing of pruning is key. Pruning at the incorrect time will negatively affect the plant's growth. Gardeners have the great responsibility to know what is best for the plant and to prune accordingly.

When we enter into a relationship with God, through Jesus Christ, God becomes our Great Gardener. Jesus is the True Vine, and we are the branches that are created to produce fruit for His glory.

Some pruning happens in winter when the plant is dormant and has stopped growing. It is a time of rest to prepare for the next season of growth. Similarly, there will be instances when we are at a time of rest in life, and the Great Gardener will determine that it is the perfect time for pruning. When life is quiet and nothing is happening, God will begin to prune us in order to prepare us for the next season of growth. While we are still and undistracted, He will remove everything that is unnecessary and excessive. By doing so, He unweights us from all the dead weight that prevents us from moving forward in life and purpose.

Some plants are best pruned right after they begin to bloom and look beautiful. The Great Gardener in His omniscience, will sometimes choose to prune us right after something great has been birthed in our lives. Just as the dream, relationship, goal, or aspiration is taking shape and blossoming into all we hoped it would be; God begins to remove what is excessive and unnecessary.

In both instances, the timing is perfect.

No one knows the perfect timing of pruning better than the gardener. We have a gardener that knows all, sees all, and is greatly invested in our fruitfulness. When we are engrafted into the True Vine, our Great Gardener will ensure that we are fruitful beyond measure. We may not always understand the timing of God's pruning, but we can always trust it because His intentions toward us are pure and His heart is overflowing with compassion for us.

God in His infinite wisdom and care for us, removes everything that hinders our growth. Let our perspective of pruning always be that of praise and thanksgiving. Praise for the opportunity to be connected, and not just attached to the True Vine, and thanksgiving for the fruitfulness that comes from the faithful and trustworthy hand of our Great Gardener.

Pruning is the blessing we may not always want, but will always need. It is an invaluable blessing that results in a stronger, more fruitful branch in the True Vine. A branch that has been lovingly pruned to produce.

For Reflection

Do I trust God to be the Great Gardener in my life?

Are there areas that I recognize as unnecessary and excessive in my life, that are hindering my growth?

How do I value fruitfulness?

What is my perspective of pruning?

For Reflection

I Want Off

But thanks be to God, who gives us the victory through our Lord Jesus Christ!
1 Corinthians 15:57 (CSB)

Some of the best childhood memories are trips to the park where we could ride bikes or fly kites. We could play on the swing, the slide, and the monkey bars and let's not forget about hopscotch and jump rope. Last but not least, there was the merry-go-round.

One person would run really fast around in a circle and then jump on to enjoy the ride. Around and around we would go and laughter and joy could be heard for miles. If the start was strong, the merry-go-round could go on for what seemed like forever. In some instances, the only way to get off before it stopped was...to jump.

Sometimes life situations can encourage us to respond in ways that serve as a defense mechanism. Personality and character traits develop as a result of the need to protect ourselves, or so we think. We begin to live, work, interact with others, and sometimes raise our children from these patterns of behavior. Every time a life situation happens, we automatically respond, how we have always responded. It is then that we board the merry-go-round that life has created, and a cycle is born.

This cycle provides a sense of security. However, if the pattern of behavior we have created does not line up with scripture, the security it provides is false, and is sure to fail us. If not corrected, it also threatens to harm the generations to come.

The realization of this faulty security system creates a question that needs to be answered:

Every time we're faced with a challenging situation, will we continue to respond the way we've always responded?

If the answer is yes, we have enrolled in a lifetime of unhealthy cycles.

But we have a choice. We can stay on the merry-go-round in unhealthy cycles or we can declare, "I want off! Off of this merry-go round and out of this cycle. "Now the question is "How?" The only way out, is the only Way in.

Jesus said to him, "I am the way, the truth, and the life. No one comes to the Father, except through me."
John 14:6 (CSB)

In relationship with God through Jesus Christ, we learn the best way to handle life. Jesus is the only way to God and He is the only way to successfully get out of cycles of unproductive patterns of behavior. The truth is, we will experience difficult times, but instead of choosing a cycle of unhealthy behaviors, created as a defense mechanism, we can make a different choice. We can choose to entrust our lives to God and rest in the fact that we are heaven's responsibility. Our Heavenly Father's care and protection of us is far better than anything we could ever do for ourselves.

He keeps you from all evil and preserves your life. He keeps his eye upon you as you come and go and always guards you.
Psalms 121: 7-8 (TLB)

I lie down and sleep, and all night long the Lord protects me.
Psalms 3:5 (GNT)

The Lord is my light and my salvation. Should I fear anyone? The Lord is a fortress protecting my life. Should I be frightened of anything?
Psalms 27:1 (CEB)

Be strong! Be fearless! Don't be afraid and don't be scared by your enemies, because the Lord your God is the one who marches with you. He won't let you down, and he won't abandon you.
Deuteronomy 31:6 (CEB)

The process to change unproductive patterns of behavior is not always easy. It is, however, necessary for us to properly guard our hearts and make forward progress. We have to make the choice to say "I want off!" and jump out of unhealthy cycles.

Let us be careful not to allow life situations to alter the masterpiece God has created us to be. We are not victims of life. We are victorious in the One that is life, Jesus Christ.

But thanks be to God, who gives us the victory through our Lord Jesus Christ!
1 Corinthians 15:57 (CSB)

For Reflection

Do I have behavior patterns that are falsely serving as a defense mechanism?

Are there unhealthy cycles that are operating in my life and in the lives of those closest to me?

Are there areas of my life that I need to entrust to the care of God?

For Reflection

Remember What You've Seen

He is your praise and glory; He is your God, who has done for you these great and awesome things which you have seen with your own eyes.
Deuteronomy 10:21 (AMP)

When we choose to walk in relationship with God daily, we have the blessed opportunity to build history with Him. From that history, we are able to recount what the Lord has done in times past. This is a blessing because sometimes what we see in our present can cause concern. In such cases, it is helpful to look back. It's helpful to review our history.

He is your praise and glory; He is your God, who has done for you these great and awesome things which you have seen with your own eyes.
Deuteronomy 10:21 (AMP)

After we review our history with God, we are ready to speak life and truth to our situation.

"That's right God! I remember when you provided for me."

"God, you've always been faithful. Your will is perfect and you will see me through this."

"God, we have history together. I remember what you've done. I've seen it with my own eyes."

If what we see today is concerning, we have to remember what we've seen God do in the past. Doing so will align our expectation of God's performance in this current situation.

Let's pray.

God,
I choose not to focus on what I see, but what I've seen. God we have history together. You have proven to be faithful time and time again. I remember what you've done in the past. Everything you've done has been great and awesome. I've seen it with my own eyes. You never change, therefore I expect you to do it again.

In Jesus' name,
Amen.

Upon God alone, O my soul, rest peacefully; for my expectation is from him.
Psalms 62:5 (DARBY)

For Reflection

What are three things that I remember that God has done for me in the past?

How can those memories strengthen my faith in my current situation?

For Reflection

Grace In This Place

Three times I pleaded with the Lord about this, that it should leave me. But he said to me, "My grace is sufficient for you, for my power is made perfect in weakness." Therefore I will boast all the more gladly of my weaknesses, so that the power of Christ may rest upon me.
2 Corinthians 12:8-9 (ESV)

Paul had been given a thorn in his flesh. The scripture passage describes him asking God to remove the thorn three times, to which God simply replies "My grace is sufficient."

There has been plenty of discussion regarding what Paul's thorn was, specifically. All can agree that the thorn created significant discomfort. Regardless of the type of discomfort, it was significant enough to ask for relief three times.

On that point, we can all relate to Paul. We have all experienced discomfort, of great magnitude, that caused us to ask God to remove it. Like Paul, sometimes God's response to us will be:

"My child, right here in this place, my grace is sufficient."
Grace: The favor of Christ that assists and strengthens his followers. A favor that serves to bear their troubles.

The grace of God is more than enough for all of our thorny situations. It will help and strengthen us when our weakness seems unbearable. In fact, the scripture reveals that His power is made perfect in our weakness. When we rely on the grace of God in every thorny place; not only are we strengthened to handle it, the power of God is perfected. What a gift.

When the will of God allows a thorn into our lives, let us lift our hands and declare to our Father:

"I want your perfected power to rest on me. I choose to rest in your grace in this place."

For Reflection

What area(s) of my life have I viewed as thorns?

Am I willing to trust God to strengthen me with his grace in those thorny places?

For Reflection

Fill In The Blank

If I speak in the tongues of men and of angels, but have not love, I am a noisy gong or a clanging cymbal. And if I have prophetic powers, and understand all mysteries and all knowledge, and if I have all faith, so as to remove mountains, but have not love, I am nothing. If I give away all I have, and if I deliver up my body to be burned, but have not love, I gain nothing. Love is patient and kind; love does not envy or boast; it is not arrogant or rude. It does not insist on its own way; it is not irritable or resentful; it does not rejoice at wrongdoing, but rejoices with the truth. Love bears all things, believes all things, hopes all things, endures all things.
1 Corinthians 13:1-7 (ESV)

The scripture reminds us about the value and importance of love. Regardless of our material possessions, spiritual gifts, and good works; if we don't have love, we are bankrupt.

If we compare ourselves to another person, we can be guilty of incorrectly believing that we are living the most accurate representation of love.

" Compared to _____ I'm definitely a loving person."

" I'm nicer than _____."

" I do more than _____."

However, the best way to demonstrate love correctly, is not to compare ourselves to others, but to scripture. The best way to align our actions with scripture, is to fill in the blank.

Let's do it together. Enter your name to fill in the blanks below.

_____ is patient and kind; _____ does not envy or boast; _____ is not arrogant or rude. _____ does not insist on its own way; _____ is not irritable or resentful; _____ does not rejoice at wrongdoing, but _____ rejoices with the truth. _____ bears all things, believes all things, hopes all things, endures all things.

1 Corinthians 13 defines love. It is the standard of what love looks like and there are no exceptions. Life is filled with relationships of all kinds. Relationships that are easy, relationships that are complex, and everything in between. There are relationships that are easier to demonstrate love in than others. The truth is that it doesn't matter. As a Christian, it doesn't matter if the relationship is easy or hard. Love God's way is the only currency for how we relate to people. We don't owe man retaliation, we only owe love.

Owe nothing to anyone—except for your obligation to love one another. If you love your neighbor, you will fulfill the requirements of God's law.
Romans 13:8 (NLT)

Dear God,

Forgive us if we have measured our demonstration of love by comparing ourselves to others. Thank you for your unending, unfailing, matchless love toward us. From this day forward, help us to remember to fill in the blank, so we can live the love written in 1 Corinthians 13.

In Jesus' name,
Amen

For Reflection

When is a time that I remember God loving me in the way described in 1 Corinthians 13?

What opportunities are present in my life to demonstrate love according to 1 Corinthians 13?

For Reflection

Forgive, It's All They Had To Give

Make allowance for each other's faults, and forgive anyone who offends you. Remember, the Lord forgave you, so you must forgive others.
Colossians 3:13

What if you needed $1000 and your loved one gave you $200? That $200 was the very last of the money they possessed. Although it was 100% of what they had, it doesn't change the fact that you still needed an additional $800. Likely, you would be grateful for them giving you all they had, although it didn't fully meet your need.

What if the person that hurt or disappointed you didn't intentionally set out to neglect, abandon, or reject you? What if they gave you 100% of what they had, even if it was not enough to meet your need, emotionally? When people are filled with unhealed and unresolved hurt, that's what they have to give.

It's not an excuse for the pain that your heart feels but it's a perspective to help let go and move forward. God is able to heal all hurt. He desires to fill you with His love, so that you can give the love that you may not have received to others. You may not have received it from who owed it to you. However, when you enter into a relationship with God, you are heaven's responsibility, and your heavenly Father will take it from here.

For Reflection

If I discovered that the person responsible for my pain didn't hurt me intentionally, would it be easier for me to forgive?

Do I believe that God desires and is able to heal every area that I hurt? Am I willing to release my pain to God right now?

Oftentimes, the most difficult apology to accept is the one we don't receive. Will I choose to forgive without an apology?

For Reflection

I Forgave The Man Who Raped Me

But I say to you who are willing to hear: Love your enemies. Do good to those who hate you. Bless those who curse you. Pray for those who mistreat you.
Luke 6: 27-28 (NET)

When I was fifteen I was raped. The waves of emotion seemed impossible to describe at the time. In the flood of emotions, I could identify shock, embarrassment, fear, and shame. Once the news reached my family, the journey began, at the police station. I remember walking into the police station and being directed to a room that looked a lot like what I'd seen on television. I spoke with detectives, recounting the entire story with great detail, for what seemed like hours. When leaving the police station, I remember squinting because the sunlight hurt my right eye. It was almost swollen shut from a broken blood vessel and what seemed to be an unceasing flow of tears.

The physical and emotional pain I felt in that moment, seemed to take my breath away. The weeks to come would be filled with more talks with detectives and finally a trip to the courthouse. I had rehearsed this event so.. many… times. My prayers were that I wouldn't have to say it anymore, especially in the presence of the one responsible for my pain. We arrived for court and I was asked to wait in a separate area as deliberations began. I sat in front of a window that was a clear view of blue sky and white clouds. While the legal team deliberated, I prayed. While looking out of a window that was a perfect contrast of what was going on in my mind and heart, I prayed. For hours, quietly, repeatedly. One simple prayer, "Lord, please, I don't want to go in there. I don't want to tell this story again."

The lawyer came to us and said a lot, but I only heard two words, "It's over." God answered. I didn't have to tell the story again. The judge ruled, and I could begin to move forward with life. However, after this, I was uncertain on which way was forward.

For a long time, I didn't tell the story. I didn't talk about it. Except to God, a lot.
I knew that I was loved by my heavenly Father but I hurt so badly.
"God, did I do something wrong?"
"God, I'm angry."
"God, my heart hurts."
"God, I feel alone and worthless."

In the months and years to follow I began to experience for myself the power of God's love for me. When I read His word, it healed my heart, and saved my life. I would not have survived, had I not had the living word of God. He spoke to me through His word, in one of the darkest times of my life.

When I thought I was worthless, He told me I was His poetry.
For we are his workmanship, having been created in Christ Jesus for good works that God prepared beforehand so we may do them.
Ephesians 2:10 (NET)

The word workmanship in the original language of this scripture is poiema, which is where the word poem originates. How amazing to learn that I was created as the poetry of God.

He answered the pain in my heart with His nearness.

The Lord is near the brokenhearted; he delivers those who are discouraged.
Psalms 34:18 (NET)

After receiving his healing. He answered the questions, "What now? How will this affect my life?"

And we know that all things work together for good for those who love God, who are called according to his purpose.
Romans 8:28 (NET)

He was faithful in every step of my healing with His comfort, patience, and loving kindness toward me. However, the process was not complete.

But I say to you who are willing to hear: Love your enemies. Do good to those who hate you. Bless those who curse you. Pray for those who mistreat you.
Luke 6:27-28 (NET)

Whew! Wow God! Mistreatment does not seem to accurately describe this situation. However, it actually does. To be mistreated is to be treated badly. I was raped and I was treated very badly.

Because I value my relationship with God, I didn't want to be found guilty of embracing all the comforting scriptures but not this challenging one.

How? What do I pray for the man who raped me?
I asked God to allow me to see him with His eyes, and not mine.

Dear God,
I forgive him. I'm asking that you forgive him. Please save him! I pray that He comes to the saving knowledge of Jesus Christ. Let this mistake not derail the destiny you designed for his life.
In Jesus' name I pray,
Amen

That prayer was the most difficult and humbling prayer I'd ever prayed. It changed my heart. The last person I thought I'd pray for was my rapist. However, God showed me, myself. I have made mistakes. I have sinned. I have missed the mark and I NEED GOD! I need His forgiveness. The sin I commit is not less sinful than the sin committed against me.

My responsibility is to love from my experience with a loving and forgiving God. As a result, I did not have a right to hold on to my hurt and unforgiveness.

Several years later, I saw him. I wondered what I would do, or how I'd feel, if this moment ever happened. My response? Tears. This time, they were tears of gratitude because when I saw him, he was at a worship service. I never saw him again, but by faith, I believe that God answered my prayers.

Forgive. It's time.

For Reflection

Is there hurt in my heart caused by someone?

Have I forgiven that person or persons?

Have I prayed for that person or persons?

For Reflection

Glory On Display

Well, whatever you do, whether it's eating or drinking or anything else, do it all so as to bring glory to God.
1 Corinthians 10:31 (CJB)

Becoming a Christian is not asking God to align Himself with our life and plans. It is surrendering our life and plans to Him. We align ourselves to His purpose, the purpose of heaven. Our purpose in life becomes making Him known, to show forth His glory to the world.

Glory: great honor, praise, value, wonder, and splendor.
A weighty manifestation of God's greatness and presence, that is awesome to behold.

We cannot add glory to God, but we display the glory that He is, with our lifestyle. We glorify God with our life by showing the world how wonderful He is with our everyday actions.

Well, whatever you do, whether it's eating or drinking or anything else, do it all so as to bring glory to God.
1 Corinthians 10:31 (CJB)

We display His glory in how we treat people, by how we work on our jobs, with how we interact with our family, and how we respond to difficult situations.

Let your light shine before men in such a way that they may see your good deeds and moral excellence, and [recognize and honor and] glorify your Father who is in heaven.
Matthew 5:16 (AMP)

When the world looks upon us living life as Christians, the observation should be :

"There is something so beautiful about your life, no matter what is happening. What is that?"

Then our response will be "It's the beauty of God, it's His glory"

Living for God, has nothing to do with us. It's all about Him. We have the privilege of displaying the splendor, majesty, and beauty of the Most High God, through lifestyle evangelism. Our lives should be lived in such a way, that it makes the status of heaven public, so that the world can see God and share Him.

For Reflection

How can I make God known with my life?

Does my lifestyle glorify God?

For Reflection

Your Impact Is Needed

Having gifts that differ according to the grace given to us, let us use them:
Romans 12:6a (ESV)

Impact: having a strong effect on something or someone; to influence or alter.

Causing impact can be misunderstood. Some believe that in order to cause impact, one must have a lot, or be known by many. The truth is, you cause the greatest impact when you are, you; regardless of your position or possessions.

Having gifts that differ according to the grace given to us, let us use them:
Romans 12:6a (ESV)

God has placed gifts, talents, and ideas in all of us. When used under His leadership, those gifts can cause great impact in the lives of others, for the kingdom of God. However, impact cannot occur in our inactivity. This is not to say that we have to be overly busy, in order for God to be glorified, or to cause impact. It is simply important to remember that God has placed treasure in us. He wants what He has placed in us to be poured out in the Earth.

Those that need to experience God the most, may not ever step inside the comfort of a church building. However, they may experience Him through your book, business, art, talent, gift, or expertise. What's in you, could change the lives of millions of people. Even if your impact affects one single life, the ripple effect could be astronomical. Think about it. What if the treasure that's hidden in you, changes the life of the inventor of the cure for cancer?

There are several different types of people on the planet. The people that God designed you to share your gifts with, are not the same as any one of your family or friends. It is impossible to make a difference in the lives that we are called to impact, by being a replica of someone else.

The way that God designed you, is the person that the world needs. The ability to embrace your identity for impact, eliminates the need for jealousy. It also encourages the celebration of the gifts and talents of others. This is important because, although we are all different, we all have the same goal. That goal is to look like Christ and make His name great in the Earth.

There are people that need someone to make a difference in their lives, and you are that person. Embrace your identity to make a great impact. Embrace your difference, so you can make a difference. Your impact is needed.

For Reflection

What gifts and talents has God blessed me with?

Am I being a good steward of these gifts and talents?

How can I use my gifts and talents to cause impact?

Has God called me to a specific demographic of people? If so, what is it?

In what way can I make God's name great in the Earth?

For Reflection

How Will You Use What You Have Left?

Come unto me, all you that labor and are heavy laden, and I will give you rest.
Matthew 11:28 (KJ2000)

It's a new day! You wake up, ready to pick up today's to do list and be productive. The list is massive, but there is a plan. Almost, down to the minute, a blueprint is in place to get it done. Ready...set...go! Operation "Crush The To Do List" is underway. You get into your vehicle. First errand done! Second errand done! Items are being marked off the list, left and right, then it happens. The gas light comes on....Sigh.

"I'm on a roll now, I have stuff to do in a certain amount of time, and driving out of the way to the gas station is inconvenient at best."

Decision.

"Do I use the little gas I have to get to the gas station now?, or make two more stops and then go to the gas station? I have enough, right?"

Come unto me, all you that labor and are heavy laden, and I will give you rest.
Matthew 11:28 (KJ2000)

Have you ever been tired and heavy? A fatigue that you can hardly describe to someone else, because not only is your body tired; your heart is heavy, and your mind is weighted...with everything. Your strength reserve is almost empty.

With life's responsibilities staring us in the face, we feel that with the ounce of strength left, we have to keep......going. That is until exhaustion shows up, mentally and physically.

Our focus scripture offers an invitation to those that are tired and weighted. The promise is, if we go to Jesus, we get rest.

Rest: to cease from movement or labor (physical and mental); in order to recover and collect strength, and be refreshed.

When we are tired and heavy, we have to make the decision to stop and get to Jesus instead of going more places and doing more things.

Let us go to Jesus, and just be...

Be still
Be quiet
Be strengthened
Be refreshed

After all, he created us as human *be*ings.

God created all of us to do something. However, in order to complete our assignment and fulfill our purpose, we have to get the rest and refreshment we need. Making the decision to do one more thing, or make one more stop, after the gas light comes on; could be expensive. It could cause damage to key parts of the vehicle. Furthermore, the time spent towing a vehicle with no gas will be longer than the inconvenient detour to the gas station to begin with.

I know, there are a lot of things to do. It's also true that there will always be things that need to be done. Most importantly, not stopping to find rest in Jesus, is costly to our destiny. It creates delay, and causes us to be ineffective in our efforts to be productive.

Life is real, responsibilities are real, trials are real, and exhaustion is real. However, so is our destiny and purpose. We are all created to meet a specific need in the Earth. Let's not be found to be unavailable and ineffective in doing so, because we failed to go to Jesus for the necessary rest and refreshment.

Our purpose remains, even when our strength is limited. Therefore, when we find ourselves tired and weary, let us use the strength we have left, to get to Jesus. He is waiting, arms wide open, to strengthen and refresh us; so we can effectively move forward in the things we are purposed to do.

For Reflection

Right now, at this moment, am I tired and in need of rest?

What choice do I need to make to have time to spend with God to be refreshed in His presence?

For Reflection

The Secret Place: The Decision

He who dwells in the secret place of the Most High will rest in the shadow of the Almighty.
Psalms 91:1 (WEB)

In the original language of the Bible, the secret place is defined as a covering, shelter, and hiding place. Most High is a description of God being the highest in all things, in every way. There is no god or created being higher than Him.

This scripture tells of a safe place of covered shelter, that belongs to the most superior God, with the highest authority. This safe place comes with the promise of rest in God Almighty. This place, His presence, and this promise, is available with the decision to dwell.
Dwell: to live or stay as a permanent resident.

He who dwells in the secret place.....

The decision to dwell in the secret place is a decision of intentionality. It is a decision to partake in close fellowship with God, on purpose. It is a decision to live in the place of being in continual, intimate communication with the Most High God. It is a decision to enter into the place of genuine communion, and staying there.

Where we live naturally is a matter of physical location. Where we live spiritually is a matter of the position of our heart. To dwell in the secret place, is a decision to always have our hearts postured toward heaven. It is to always have our ear to the heartbeat of God. It is to earnestly desire His will and purpose, in everything we say and do.

When our heart is at home in God and we place His presence as our life's priority, we make the decision to become a permanent resident of the secret place, so we are perfectly positioned for rest in every situation. Rest, in the shadow of El Shaddai. Rest in God Almighty.

For Reflection

Have I made the decision to dwell in the secret place?

When have I experienced rest as a result of my decision to dwell in the secret place?

For Reflection

The Promise In the Wait

Yet, the strength of those who wait with hope in the Lord will be renewed. They will soar on wings like eagles. They will run and won't become weary. They will walk and won't grow tired.
Isaiah 40:31 (GW)

They will soar on wings like eagles...

Eagles are known to be able to soar at heights of 10,000 feet above the ground. The perspective is much different at this height.

When we wait on God, He will strengthen us to be able to rise above any situation. At the correct altitude, seated with Him in high places; we can view any situation from heaven's perspective.

They will run and won't become weary...

There will be times that God will cause us to make rapid moves. We may need to run in order to get where we need to be. In these situations, we can't afford the cost of weariness. The strength we receive by waiting on God, will guard us from physical or mental exhaustion during swift transitions.

They will walk and won't grow tired...

Sometimes we will be required to walk the distance and endurance is key to finishing. God's strength equips us and prevents us from becoming tired and drained while we are walking out our destiny.

If we wait, we will receive the strength necessary to respond properly to whatever life brings. We will be able rise above any situation, handle the altitude, and soar. Let us make the choice to wait on God because with His strength we cannot fail.

With His strength we will soar.

With His strength we will run.

With His strength we will walk.

With His strength we will finish…..if we wait.

For Reflection

Am I currently operating in God's strength or my own?

Am I willing to choose to wait on God and receive His strength?

For Reflection

Faith That Will Amaze

Now faith is the reality of what is hoped for, the proof of what is not seen.
Hebrews 11:1 (CSB)

The Bible records two times that Jesus is amazed.

The first instance is in the sixth chapter of Mark's gospel, when Jesus is in His hometown with his fellow countrymen. The locals in Nazareth are in Jesus' presence and able to hear the wisdom he spoke and see him perform miracles with his own hands. However, because they knew the family he'd come from, that he was a carpenter, and that he had not received formal education; he was not considered worthy to be a rabbi.

Although it was evident that the wisdom he spoke with and the power he performed miracles in was supernatural, they did not believe. As a result, his ability to perform miracles there was limited.

He was not able to do a miracle there, except that he laid his hands on a few sick people and healed them. And he was amazed at their unbelief. He was going around the villages teaching.
Mark 6:5-6 (CSB)

The second instance is in the seventh chapter of Luke's gospel where a centurion's servant is sick and near death. He heard that Jesus was near and sent a message asking Jesus to save his servant's life. Jesus was on His way to the centurion's house to heal his servant, and the centurion stopped Jesus from entering his house. He said to Jesus to "just say the word and my servant will be healed." Jesus was amazed.

Jesus heard this and was amazed at him, and turning to the crowd following him, he said, "I tell you, I have not found so great a faith even in Israel."
Luke 7:9 (CSB)

Both instances of Jesus' amazement are centered around faith; the presence and the absence of it.

In one instance, Jesus was physically present but the faith of his fellow countrymen was absent. In the other, the faith of the centurion was present although Jesus was physically absent from his situation.

Without faith, we will not be able to recognize the presence of God in our situation. However, when our faith is present, it becomes the proof that God is active in our circumstance even when we can't see Him.

Now faith is the reality of what is hoped for, the proof of what is not seen.
Hebrews 11:1 (CSB)

Let us not place our faith in the capability of our adversities, but in the character of our God that will never fail. Let's make an intentional choice to live by faith. Faith that is confident in the character of God. Faith that is proof that He will perform in our situation, even when we don't see Him. Faith that will amaze God.

So faith comes from what is heard, and what is heard comes through the message about Christ.
Romans 10:17 (CSB)

For Reflection

Where have I placed my confidence? In the character of God or the outcome of difficult life situations?

Are there areas in my life that I can increase my faith?

For Reflection

Fight The Feeling, Persevere.

Not only that, but we also rejoice in our sufferings, because we know that suffering produces perseverance; perseverance, character, and character, hope.
Romans 5:3-4 (BSB)

Oftentimes, a new year brings declarations, decisions, and a shiny new level of dedication. We feel inspired and strengthened to go after it. There's nothing like a fresh start to motivate us to action. At the beginning of the year, we are ready to set and meet goals immediately. We set goals to lose weight, gain muscle, spend more time doing one thing, less time doing another, stop a bad habit, or create a useful habit. However, what do we do when we no longer "feel" like doing what it takes to reach our goals?

The answer….. Persevere

Persevere: to persist in anything undertaken; maintain a purpose in spite of difficulty, obstacles, or discouragement; continue steadfastly.

In reality, the excitement we "feel" at the beginning of the year is not enough to become the person we know God has called us to be by the end of the year; physically, mentally, and spiritually.

There may be days when we will have to maintain our purpose to the point of what may seem like suffering. On those days we will fight the feeling to quit and…

Persevere our way to the gym.
Persevere in the process of forgiveness.
Persevere in studying to be quiet, when we are not at a loss for words
Persevere in guarding our heart
Persevere in moving forward on that business plan
Persevere in a disciplined lifestyle

Submission to becoming the person God created us to be includes suffering, but Romans tells us that the end result is hope.

Not only that, but we also rejoice in our sufferings, because we know that suffering produces perseverance; perseverance, character, and character, hope.
Romans 5:3-4 (BSB)

The journey to destiny develops us into the person we need to be, so we can properly handle the place we're going. However, we will not reach our destination by traveling the road of our emotions. In order to become all God created us to be, we have to persevere toward what's right, even when our feelings are wrong.

As we continue through the year, let's live intentionally, everyday. Let's keep the goals that God has given us to reach, in direct view. When motivation is low and challenges arise, fight the feeling to quit, and persevere... your destiny is waiting.

For Reflection

At this moment, am I as focused and motivated to meet the goals I set at the beginning of the year?

Am I persevering in areas that I don't "feel" motivated in?

Am I willing to recommit to maintaining my purpose regardless of my feelings?

For Reflection

He's Worth The Climb

The next day, when the large crowd who had come to the Passover feast heard that Jesus was coming to Jerusalem, they took branches of palm trees [in homage to Him as King] and went out to meet Him, and they began shouting and kept shouting "Hosanna! Blessed (celebrated, praised) is He who comes in the name of the Lord, even the King of Israel!"
John 12:12-13 (AMP)

Jesus entered the city of Jerusalem humbly. In peace, he rode into town on a young, unridden donkey; not a horse commonly used by war heroes. The crowd that gathered, recognized Jesus as king, and met him with palm branches. Some placed the palm branches in His path with their cloaks in biblical red carpet fashion.

Palm branches represent victory and triumph. Their use was a common expression of honor for kings in biblical times. Although the use of palm branches was common, it was not easy. The average height of a palm tree varies between 32 and 50 ft., with the tallest palm tree growing to be 230 ft. tall. This means that, at the very least, one would have to climb the height of two giraffes standing one on top of the other, just to reach the branch of a palm tree.

When honoring kings in biblical times, people were willing to climb high. Regardless of a fear of heights, they would climb. Regardless of the weather, they would climb. Regardless of the effort required, they would climb. Regardless of how they felt, they would climb. They would climb because there was a king in their presence that was worthy of honor.

We should also climb, just as those who lived in biblical times. Our climbing may not be literal, but we should climb to honor our King.

Climb: to go up with gradual or continuous progress

We honor God with our progress. However, honoring Him in this way requires us to ask hard questions.

How is our stewardship?

How is our commitment?

How well do we relate to others?

Where is progress needed in our lives?

When we take the opportunity to progress in necessary areas, we climb. We climb high, and we honor our King in the process.

Palm Sunday is the day in biblical history that marks Jesus' Triumphal Entry into Jerusalem. This entry was different from any other entry. This entry made Jesus' status as Messiah public. This entry didn't announce the arrival of just any king. This was the entry of the King of Kings. The King worthy of the greatest honor.

Regardless of what day or season it is, Iet us always choose to climb in honor of our King. Let's consider the opportunities we have to climb high in our everyday lives. Whatever the effort, whatever the sacrifice, whatever the discipline, whatever the cost, let's do it! Let's make a declaration to our King! "Lord, you are worth the climb! Your honor is far greater than my comfort."

For Reflection

What opportunities do I have in my life to climb higher by way of progressing in the necessary areas ?

For Reflection

We Can't Lose For Winning

And we know [with great confidence] that God [who is deeply concerned about us] causes all things to work together [as a plan] for good for those who love God, to those who are called according to His plan and purpose.
Romans 8:28 (AMP)

When we make a decision to enter into a relationship with God we have a promise that all things will work together for our good no matter what. However, there has been a misunderstanding surrounding this decision. It has been misunderstood that a life with God is a life without trouble, and that is not true.

The truth, according to Psalms 34:18, is that many hardships and perplexing circumstances confront the righteous, but the Lord rescues him from them all.

As Christians, the promise is not to live a life void of hard times. The promise is that we will always be rescued. We don't get to personally design the details of the rescue, but we can expect the Lord to rescue us, and that it will work together for our good.

God has been faithful to His promises in every difficult situation in my life.

When my father died, it worked for my good.
I experienced a peace that my mind could not comprehend. A peace that comforted me as I delivered his eulogy.

When I was raped, it worked for my good.
I received a new revelation of the power of forgiveness. The same forgiveness I extended is the same forgiveness I need from my heavenly father. The sin committed against me was not greater than the sins I have committed.

I have never raised my hand to volunteer for my trials, but I am so very grateful for the treasure I gained from each of them. The treasure I gained was God's promise to work everything together for my good. I know by experience that God is a God of peace, grace, and forgiveness.

Regardless of what it feels like, God always has our best interest at heart. Nothing we experience will be wasted. Although we may experience difficult situations, it will work together for our good.

We can trust Him.

He has a perfect plan for us.

We cannot lose because we are victorious in Him.

We can't lose for winning.

> *but thanks be to God, who giveth us the victory through our Lord Jesus Christ.*
> *1 Corinthians 15:57 (ASV)*

For Reflection

What are some past difficult situations that God worked together for good?

God will never change, am I willing to trust that He will give me victory in any of my current hardships?

For Reflection

I Will Be Single

Let your eyes look forward; fix your gaze straight ahead.
Proverbs 4:25 (CSB)

The way that we receive information has advanced tremendously in recent years. There was a time where obtaining information required significant effort. In some instances, we had to travel to the library to borrow a book for research. In other instances, we sought the opportunity to unlock wisdom from an in-person conversation.

Now, unlimited information is at our fingertips. Directions to a mall in another state, the weather for next week, the menu for our favorite restaurant, the location of our colleague's vacation, and the date for the next conference, are available in seconds.

Advances in technology have not only made obtaining information convenient, it has also created a wide variety of things for us to attend to. As a result, it has created an increased need to be single.
Single: exclusively attentive

In the fourth chapter of Proverbs, Solomon imparts wisdom to his son that is beneficial for all of us. In verse 25, he teaches the importance of being single.

Let your eyes look forward; fix your gaze straight ahead.
Proverbs 4:25 (CSB)

In a world that grabs our attention from every direction, we have to be intentional about fixing our gaze on God. We have to be determined not to allow the convenience the world has provided, to be catastrophic to our relationship with God.

Living and learning from convenience is not wrong. In fact, God has called some to the advancement of information technology. However, we have to remember that God is the standard. God is the reward. He is the source, and everything and everyone else is a resource.

Any information that we receive should be filtered through the word of God and His design and purpose for our life, not anyone else's life.

There are so many good things to attend to and participate in. Yet we have the responsibility to ask ourselves, if this good thing is the God thing that I've been called to.

We have to be single, exclusively attentive to God. If not, we can be subtly and unintentionally pulled away from the path and purpose that God designed for our lives.

Singleness of attention in this information age, does not happen by accident. It requires intention and an uncompromising commitment to guard our gaze. It requires both action and declaration against distraction.

"I will be single in my pursuit of God"

"I will be single in my calling and assignment"

"I will be single about my forward progress, and not distracted by my past"

"I will be single in my resolve to give back to God what He has placed in me"

"I will be single in the stewardship of my time, talent, and treasure."

Let us be balanced and sober with the information we are offered. Let us be intentional about guarding our gaze and avoiding distraction. Although we are offered so much to attend to, let us remain exclusive in our attention to God. He is the only one true and living God. He is the only one that gave His son to die in our place. Therefore, He alone is worthy of our undivided attention and our commitment of singleness.

For Reflection

How does having information at my fingertips affect my daily decisions?

Are there any ways that the advances in technology encourage my singleness to God?

What guards do I have in place to protect me from distraction? Am I single?

For Reflection

Nevertheless...I'll Keep It

saying, "Father, if it is Your will, take this cup away from Me; nevertheless not My will, but Yours, be done."
Luke 22:42 (NKJV)

Jesus was assigned to come to Earth to die for our sins. The night before he was set to complete this assignment, He prayed in the Garden of Gethsemane:

saying, "Father, if it is Your will, take this cup away from Me; nevertheless not My will, but Yours, be done."
Luke 22:42 (NKJV)

In His prayer, Jesus made a request and a declaration. When His assignment poured a cup of suffering, Jesus requested that the cup pass from Him. However, His request was immediately followed with a declaration. That declaration was simple. Nevertheless. Nevertheless: nonetheless; notwithstanding; however; in spite of that.

Jesus declared, "nevertheless not My will, but Yours, be done."

God! In spite of that request I made, I want what you want, not what I want.

God! In spite of me requesting the cup to pass from me, I'll keep it, if that is what I need to do, in order to complete the assignment you have given me.

Nevertheless.

We may not have been assigned to sacrifice our lives as Jesus was, however, completing our assignment will cost us something.

It may cost us time.

It may cost us money.

It may cost our comfort.

It may cost our tears.

In spite of that.... God still deserves our "yes!"

He deserves for us to live life in complete devotion to Him.

Like Jesus, we must choose to declare, "nevertheless!"

Nevertheless, I will walk out my calling.

Nevertheless, I will end the generational cycles in my family.

Nevertheless, I will complete my assignment.

Nevertheless, I'll keep it.

I will keep my cup.

Nevertheless, God I will do your will.

Then an angel appeared to Him from heaven, strengthening Him.
Luke 22:43 (NKJV)

After Jesus made the declaration for God's will to be done, an angel came and strengthened Him.

God is aware of the cost of your assignment. He is a good Father and is faithful to supply all of our needs, including strength. He simply desires for us to say yes to His will. In turn, He will provide the necessary strength to complete all that He has assigned us to do.

Any assignment completed for the kingdom of God is worth the cost, no matter how great. It's worth it because God thought that we were worth it, when He gave His son Jesus to die for us.
Completing our individual assignments is our opportunity and responsibility in sharing the message of Jesus Christ. No one else can complete our assignment. It is our responsibility.

In spite of it all, let us choose to make the declaration. "Nevertheless, I'll keep it! I'll keep my cup and I will complete my assignment in the Earth, no matter the cost."

God,
My assignment is not always easy. It has and will cost me to complete it. Whatever the cost God, you have my yes! Nevertheless, I gladly accept the assignment you've given me. Thank you for choosing me. Thank you in advance for the strength to complete it.

In Jesus' name,
Amen

For Reflection

What has God assigned me to do?

What is the cost of this assignment?

Am I committed to completing the assignment regardless of any challenge or obstacle that may arise?

God, thank you for choosing me to _____. Today I make a "Nevertheless" commitment. "I will complete my assignment in the Earth, no matter the cost."

For Reflection

Our Perfect Example

Therefore, my dear brothers and sisters, be steadfast, immovable, always excelling in the Lord's work, because you know that your labor in the Lord is not in vain.
1 Corinthians 15:58 (CSB)

Paul is writing to call to remembrance the importance of resurrection, specifically the resurrection of Christ. In his letter to the Corinthian church, Paul reiterates that the death and resurrection of Christ is the foundation of Christianity. At the end of chapter fifteen, Paul encourages them to be steadfast, immovable, and always excelling in the Lord's work.

Steadfast: fixed in purpose

Jesus was steadfast, fixed in purpose. His purpose was to come to Earth, die on a cross, be buried, and rise from the grave and He never wavered in His purpose. He lived on Earth, fully God and fully man. In fixed purpose, He experienced hunger, pain, grief, and rejection. His magnificent purpose made eternal life available to all who believe.

Immovable: Firmly persistent

In death, he was immoveable. He was firmly persistent to stay on the cross, and die for the sins of humanity. In His deity, he could have called for angels to rescue him, but He did not.

Excel: to surpass others; do extremely well

The work of the cross, excels all other gods. There is no god that compares to the one true and living God. There is no other god that came to Earth, lived, died for our sins, and rose again from the dead. There is no other way to be saved than through Jesus. The very character of God surpasses all other gods.

Jesus has given us a perfect example. He was steadfast, fixed in purpose; as He experienced all the challenges that come with living as a human on Earth. He was immovable, firmly persistent; on the cross until death. He excelled all other gods, in His resurrection from the dead.

He has given us an example of how to remain fixed in purpose and firmly persistent, no matter what. He has shown us that being steadfast and immovable is possible. He demonstrated the importance of excelling in God's work. If Jesus did not excel by raising from the dead, there would be no gift of eternal life available for us.

Let us be steadfast in our purpose. Let us be immovable in fulfilling God's agenda on Earth. Let us always excel in the work that we've been called to, because our obedience affects more than just us.

There will be challenges. There may even be tears. Nevertheless, in Christ there will always be victory. With God all things are possible. We can be confident in this, because Jesus did it first.

He is our perfect example.

For Reflection

Are there areas in my life for me to become steadfast?

Are there areas in my life for me to be immovable?

How can I excel in the Lord's work?

How can I apply Jesus' example to my everyday living?

For Reflection

Finish

I have fought a good fight, I have finished my course, I have kept the faith.
2 Timothy 4:7 (KJV)

In reflection, we may remember a combination of experiences during our lifetime. There may have been times of great joy, deep sadness, unexplainable laughter, and everything in between.

Some of us may reflect and find great accomplishment; where others of us have yet to accomplish our goals. In honesty, our reasons for lack of accomplishment vary. For one of us, it may be a life changing event or circumstance that changed the trajectory of life. For others of us, it may be a lack of motivation. Whatever the reason, the reality is that we are now at a point of decision.

Time has passed, yet time remains. Although we don't know how much time remains, there are questions that must be answered.

What were God's instructions for me?

Did I follow those instructions?

If the answer is yes to the second question, I am so excited for you and celebrate your progress and accomplishments.

If the answer is no to the second question, there are more questions.

Have God's instructions for me expired?

Does the presence of challenge or the absence of motivation cancel those instructions?

If the answer to both questions was no, the encouragement is to finish strong.

We could have lengthy discussion surrounding the reasons that God's instructions were not followed. Instead, let's get up, remember the instructions, and finish strong.

This life will provide several reasons for us not to do what we've been instructed to do. Instead of focusing on those reasons, let's focus on the one reason we should; we were born for this. Literally. We were fashioned by God with a treasure locked inside of us. The treasure will only be unlocked by following instructions. One act of obedience at a time, leading us right into our destiny.

There is still time to finish and complete the instructions that God has given to us. Let us not be distracted by what hasn't happened. Instead, let's focus on what can happen. Let us remember the instruction, refocus our obedience, and run toward the finish line.

Finish. Strong.

For Reflection

Have I followed every instruction that God has given me?

What step can I take today to move in obedience to what God has instructed me to do?

What is a reasonable deadline to set for finishing this assignment?

For Reflection

Pour

I'm reminded of your authentic faith, which first lived in your grandmother Lois and your mother Eunice. I'm sure that this faith is also inside you.
2 Timothy 1:5 (CSB)

In Paul's final letter, he personally addresses Timothy, his son in the ministry. In the featured scripture, Paul speaks of the authentic faith of Timothy's mother and grandmother that was poured out in Timothy's life.

Pour: express one's feelings or thoughts in a full and unrestrained way

Lois and Eunice expressed their feelings and thoughts about God, in a full and unrestrained way, in the lives that they lived before Timothy. It was their pour from Timothy's infancy that contributed to the authentic faith that fueled his calling as a minister of the gospel. It is because of their pour, that Timothy was able to go on to live out the meaning of his name, "honoring God".

As we live a life that fully expresses our feelings and thoughts about God, we have the opportunity and responsibility to pour our faith into the lives of others. Our pour can change the trajectory of a person's life and ministry. Our pour can help to fulfill the work of the kingdom of God. Our pour can help bring people to the saving knowledge of Jesus Christ.

Eunice and Lois' names are only mentioned once in the Bible. The one time their names are written, is with regard to the pour of faith they made into Timothy's life. All of us have a calling and a work to complete for the kingdom of God. That calling may not cause our name to be known, but it should always result in God's name being known.

Our callings may be different, but we are all called to intentionally pour our faith into those that are assigned to us, just as Lois and Eunice did with Timothy. Even if our name is never recognized, we must pour, because the kingdom of God is at hand.

Then he said to them, "Go into all the world and preach the gospel to all creation.
Mark 16:15 (CSB)

For Reflection

Who has poured their faith into me?

How has my life been affected by the pour of others?

Who have I been assigned to pour into?

For Reflection

It Is Good

It is good to praise the Lord. God Most High, it is good to praise your name. It is good to sing about your love in the morning and about your faithfulness at night.
Psalms 92:1-2 (ERV)

Dear God,

We approach the throne of grace, not with hands extended,
but with hands lifted in praise to Your High Name.
We praise You because nothing that exists is greater than You!
We praise You because You are highest in rank, and You alone, reign supreme!
We arise early to honor You with the praise of our lips because of Your unfailing love!
We praise You God for Your loyalty to us all day long, as You keep us, provide for us, and guide us!
We will live in a posture of praise, in gratitude for Your lovingkindness toward us.
Regardless of our situation, it is always good to praise Your name.
Our situations may change, seasons may change, but You never will.

If things seem bad, it is good.
If people walk away, it is good.
When things are going well, it is good.

It is always good to praise Your name because You are always good, and for that we are eternally grateful.

In Jesus' name,
Amen

Acknowledgements

God, I am absolutely nothing without you. I am forever grateful to you for giving your son to die in my place, so that I may live eternally with you in death, and live abundantly in relationship with you in life. You have my complete "yes." All that I am is because of you and all that I do is for you. My sole desire in life is for you to be glorified and to advance your kingdom agenda on Earth. I love you with my whole heart.

C.D., my husband, my promise, my love. I honor you and thank you for your willingness to go above and beyond to love, protect, provide, and care for our family. It is truly astonishing and a tremendous blessing. Thank you so much for your encouragement and unfailing support in all that I do. I love and appreciate you greatly.

Josiah and Jacob, it is an honor and a privilege to be your mother and to see you mature into the men of God you were created to be. It is my daily prayer and declaration over your life that you will know God intimately, and that His purpose and calling for your life will come to pass without delay. I pray that the anointing on your lives will travel generations, leaving a legacy of men that know God and live for Him wholeheartedly without wavering or compromise. I love you both so much.

Taylor, I am grateful to God for the gift, honor, and privilege it has been to be a part of your life. I pray that you never forget how much God loves you and how much your life is an example of God's miraculous power to overcome all things. Continue to grow and thrive in all that you do.
I love you.

Mom, thank you so much for always loving and supporting me with the full capacity of your heart. I honor the journey you have walked with God and the testimony of all that you have experienced and overcome. Your best days are ahead of you. God has an amazing future planned for you, and I am excited and waiting in great expectation to see it all unfold in your favor. I love you so much.

Acknowledgements

C.D. Fortson, Jr. and Rosalind Fortson, my parents in love. Thank you for loving me as your very own daughter. It has been a true gift to my heart and so very appreciated. I love you both.

Alesia, my aunt. You have been a consistent and strong presence in my life. Your quiet disposition has spoken loud lessons to my life and my heart that are invaluable. I am honored to be your namesake and grateful for your love and support.

Lacretia Thomas, my big sister. My well being is always a top priority for you and I appreciate you for it. Thank you for your love and support that reaches beyond the 1700 miles that separate us, I love you.

Apostle Larry B. Aiken and Pastor Olivia C.Q. Aiken, I honor your integral, genuine, and sacrificial love and leadership over the last 27 years. I am certain that the trajectory of my life would be gravely different without it. My gratitude for your presence and prayers in my life is indescribable, invaluable, and immensely appreciated. Thank you, I love you both.

Sincere covenant friendship is an invaluable and precious gift that should be treasured. Pastor Calandra Sumpter, Elder Monique Hardman, Pastor Casandra Simington, Pastor Kaylette Blunt, Minister Kreasha Williams, First Lady Robbin Roustic, Melanie Wages, Lashanda Grant, and LaTasha Hicks, thank you. The value you carry in my heart is priceless. I treasure, honor, and appreciate you for your presence and purpose in my life. I love you all.

Debra Payne and Patricia Moss, thank you. I am forever grateful to God for your Titus 2 presence in my life. I will never forget your love, kindness, support, guidance, and intercession on my behalf. Thank you, I love you.

Acknowledgements

To my Memorial Church International family in Christ. I cannot name you all individually, but please know that your prayers and tangible expressions of love and support are genuinely cherished, loved, appreciated, and will never be forgotten. I love you all.

Aisha Brown with Life's Productions. The incomparable value you add to the exciting, arduous, and life changing editing process is nothing short of amazing. Not only did you edit but you listened, encouraged, and prayed with me throughout the entire process and I am forever grateful. You are truly walking in your God ordained purpose and it is evident. Keep going, greater is coming.

The absence of your name in print, is not the absence of gratitude and appreciation in my heart for everyone for your love and support in any and all capacities. Thank you so much. I pray heaven's choice blessings be yours forever.

About The Author

Arlesia Fortson is a native of Kansas City, MO where she currently resides with her husband C.D. of 18 years and their two sons Josiah and Jacob. She graduated high school from Lincoln College Preparatory Academy and furthered her education at Rockhurst University where she earned a Bachelor of Arts degree in Psychology and a Master's Degree in Occupational Therapy. Arlesia has practiced occupational therapy since 2005 and has served critically ill patients in the intensive care setting, specifically those that are undergoing transplantation of the liver, kidney, pancreas, and bone marrow for the majority of her career. Her passion for helping others, however, reaches beyond the bedside of her patients. When not treating patients, she has held workshops and facilitated classes supporting her passion to help other make and achieve goals, succeed in time management, and create and execute an effective budget.

Arlesia has been a faithful and committed member of Memorial Church International in Kansas City, Missouri, under the leadership of Apostle Larry B. Aiken and Pastor Olivia C.Q. Aiken since 1995. Since that time she has had the opportunity to serve in several capacities including as a member of the First Touch Ministry, and as a deaconess and altar assistant. She has taught bible study and Sunday School classes, as well as Financial Peace University classes. She also serves in the music ministry as member and president of the Sanctuary Choir. Arlesia is a licensed and ordained minister of the gospel that accepted her call to ministry in 2013. She now serves as an elder on the Minister's Alliance at Memorial Church International. In 2017, God called her to create Wellspring Expressions, a Christian blog that exists to equip women to cultivate a strong relationship with God through encouragement, prayer, and bible study. In 2022 Arlesia published her first book, a devotional entitled, The Water and The Well: Encounters With God.

The sole purpose of all that Arlesia does is to glorify God and advance His kingdom agenda on Earth. She loves God with her whole heart and lives to fulfill the call of ministry upon her life, first to her husband and children, and then to women by way of prayer, teaching, writing, healing, and prophecy.

Connect With Us

www.wellspringexpressions.com

- Wellspring Expressions
- wellspringexpressions
- @WellExpressions
- @WellExpressions
- Wellspring Expressions
- Wellspring Expressions

Scripture Index

Everlasting Valentine:	John 3:16
Let's Start Here:	Ephesians 3:17-19
The Original Document:	2 Corinthians 5:17
What If They Were Wrong?:	Hebrew 4:12
May I Borrow Your Pen?:	Psalms 45:1, Proverbs 18:21, Romans 8:18, Proverbs 4:23, Psalms 34:19
Make A Right Turn When It Hurts?	Matthew 22:36-37; Proverbs 4:23
176:	Psalms 119:1, 2, 9, 11, 28, 45, 50, 59, 66, 93, 98, 165, 105
The Condition Is Not The Counselor:	John 5: 1-9, Proverbs 24:6, Psalms 139: 1-2
The Plumb Line:	Proverbs 30:5, 2 Timothy 3:16-17
Mary's Choice	Luke 10:38-42
Press Forward There's More:	Philippians 3:12-14
Presents or Presence	Philippians 4:19, Matthew 7:11, Psalms 27:8, Psalms 34:10, Psalms 27:4
Go Back	Luke 2:41-52, James 4:8
I'm Here	Psalms 139:7-10, Psalms 16:11, Nehemiah 8:10, Psalms 46:1, Philippians 3:13-14
Who Is My Mother?	Genesis 1:26-28a, Psalms 27:10, Psalms 68:5-6, Matthew 12:47-50, John 13:35
An Encounter With God: The Remedy For Our Negative Experience	Philippians 4:6-7, Isaiah 43:18-19
Trust	John 4: 4-26
God Is: Immutable	Psalms 37:25, Psalms 33:11, Deuteronomy 31:8
Plan B	Jeremiah 29:11
If You Say So	Luke 5:1-7
The Outcome	John 14:1, Revelation 22:13
What Will You Call It?	Genesis 22: 1-14
In Conclusion	Ecclesiastes 7:8a, Psalms 86:10
Thank You!	Psalm 56:12, Psalm 100:4, Ephesians 5:20, Psalm 28:7, Colossians 2:7, Colossians 3:15, Colossians 4:2, 1 Thessalonians 5:18, 1 Chronicles 16:8, 1 Chronicles 16:34, Psalm 92:1, Psalm 109:30, Psalm 136:4, Revelation 7:12, 1 Timothy 1:12, 1 Corinthians 15:57, Psalm 69:30, Hebrews 12:28, 2 Corinthians 9:15, Psalm 68:19
Love: Reverence and Obedience	Matthew 22: 36-38, John 14:15, Ephesians 4:26, Romans 12:19, Philippians 4:8

Scripture Index

The Great Gardener	John 15:1-2
I Want Off	John 14:6, Psalms 121: 7-8, Psalms 3:5, Psalms 27:1, Deuteronomy 31:6, 1 Corinthians 15:57
Remember What You've Seen	Deuteronomy 10:21, Psalms 62:5
Grace In This Place	2 Corinthians 12:8-9
Fill In The Blank	1 Corinthians 13:1-7, Romans 13:8
Forgive, It's All They Had To Give	Collosians 3:13
I Forgave The Man Who Raped Me	Ephesians 2:10, Psalms 34:18, Romans 8:28, Luke 6:27-28
Glory On Display	1 Corinthians 10:11, Matthew 5:16
Your Impact Is Needed	Romans 12:6
How Will You Use What You Have Left?	Matthew 11:28
The Secret Place	Psalms 91:1
The Promise In The Wait	Isaiah 40:31
Faith That Will Amaze	Mark 6:1-6, Luke 7: 1-10, Hebrews 11:1, Romans 10:17
Fight The Feeling, Persevere	Romans 5:3-4
He's Worth The Climb	John 12:12-13
We Can't Lose For Winning	Romans 8:28, Psalms 34:18, 1 Corinthians 15:57
I Will Be Single	Proverbs 4:25
Nevertheless, I'll Keep It	Luke 22:42-43
Our Perfect Example	1 Corinthians 15:58, Matthew 19:26
Finish	2 Timothy 4:7
Pour	2 Timothy 1:5, 2 Timothy 3:14-15, Mark 16:15
It Is Good:	Psalms 92:1-2

www.ingramcontent.com/pod-product-compliance
Lightning Source LLC
Chambersburg PA
CBHW081204170426
43197CB00018B/2914